GETTING READY TO TEACH SECOND GRADE

By Kimberly Seto

Photos by Bruce Hazelton

Illustrated by Cary Pillo

Rosalie Cochran

Sandy Hutchinson

We warmly thank the community of the Fern Avenue School of Torrance, California, especially Mrs. Rosalie Cochran, principal; Mrs. Sandy Hutchinson, second-grade teacher; and students, parents, and caregivers of Mrs. Hutchinson's second-grade class.

Project Manager: Barbara G. Hoffman
Editor: Barbara G. Hoffman
Book Design: Anthony D. Paular
Cover Design: Anthony D. Paular
Pre-Press Production: Daniel Willits

FS122004 Getting Ready to Teach Second Grade
All rights reserved—Printed in the U.S.A.
23740 Hawthorne Blvd.
Torrance, CA 90505

Let us put our minds together and see what life we can make for our children.

—Tatanba Iotanko (Sitting Bull) 1877

CHAPTER ONE: INTRODUCTION

Second graders amaze, inspire, and encourage me. At work each day I am greeted by smiling children full of energy, eager to learn. My classes have taught me a lot about how children learn and about being an important human being. Second grade is when students refine their developing skills in reading and writing and lay the foundation for their lifelong understanding and use of mathematics.

Give students choices. Whenever students are asked to choose, they have ownership of their work and are more motivated to get the work done, whatever it may be. Teach students to be self-managed learners. These learners take responsibility for their own learning and pursue their own interests.

THE SECOND-GRADE STUDENT

During second grade, students generally have their seventh or their eighth birthdays. Typical second-grade students are:

- eager to please, seeking adult and peer approval

- in need of praise and encouragement

- producing things to win recognition

- active and learn by doing

- sensitive to classmates' needs

- creative, imaginative, and fun

- mastering new physical skills

- growing taller (approximately 2-1/2" per year)

- developing their muscles and becoming stronger

1

- comparing themselves to peers

- full of energy

- reaching out for acceptance

- needing family support

- concerned about fairness and taking turns

- talkative and tending to tattle

- worried about making new friends

- starting to work cooperatively

- willing to share their ideas and work

- developing their identities

- learning that words and pictures represent real objects

- able to talk about present and past events

- comprehending more words than they are able to use

- increasing word usage at a rapid rate

- full of questions

- learning the difference between reality and fantasy

- able to concentrate attention for longer periods of time

- capable of sorting objects by attributes such as size and shape

- able to do some complex thinking and decision making

- using strategies to solve problems

- improving their memory skills

OVERVIEW OF THE SECOND-GRADE CURRICULUM

This section is presented in alphabetical order by content area. The sequence is Language Arts, Mathematics, Multicultural Education, Physical Education, Science and Health, Social Studies, Technology, and Visual and Performing Arts (which includes Music).

In this overview section you will read about the concepts that are to be addressed in second grade. In Chapter Two—Bringing the Curriculum to Life—you will find a list of skills by content area generally accepted as appropriate for second grade. Following the lists of skills, you will find activities that you can use to teach the skills.

The content and curriculum information presented in this book is provided as a reference. It is not intended to replace your school or district's course of study or curriculum guides. As additional references, you should read the standards published by national teacher organizations such as the National Council of Teachers of Mathematics. Your school or district resource centers will probably have copies of the National Standards documents you can use as references.

Parts of the curriculum sections of this book are based on the Standards of the National Council of the Teachers of Mathematics, the National Council of the Teachers of English, and the National Research Council of the National Academy of Sciences. Other references used are state frameworks and school district curricula from Illinois, California, Nebraska, Massachusetts, Washington, and New York.

Education is not the filling of a pail, but the lighting of a fire.

—William Butler Yeats

Language Arts

Language Arts is a broad area of the curriculum which includes reading, writing, listening, and speaking. Through these processes, students express what they know, what they think, and what they value about the world. They make connections between information they know and information they don't know.

Your school or district may have adopted textbooks or other language arts programs that include grammar, spelling, activity and workbooks, or there may be specific guidelines you are expected to follow. Check with the curriculum coordinator or principal at your school before the school year begins.

Concepts

- Language is used to communicate ideas and to express our feelings.

- Language allows us to express our life experiences in general, and with reference to specific ideas and values that we can name.

- Language allows us to share what we know and what we understand about ourselves and those around us.

Developing the Art of Language

Three components are important to developing the art of language in your classroom. The first is the use of literature, the second is easy access to many books and other educational media, and the third is an emphasis on writing as a process.

Literature

Books create a bridge between the "real world" and your classroom, and between different curricular areas. Good literature makes any information interesting and accessible.

Library Media Resources

Your students should have regular access to a variety of materials from which they can select according to their interests. Develop a classroom library as well as use the resources of the school and local public libraries.

Writing

The process of speech-to-print is crucial to language development. The writing process includes several stages—prewriting, drafting, receiving responses, revising, editing, and in many cases, postwriting. Through the writing process students develop their writing and related skills. They also improve their spoken language by discussing their work and the work of others.

- The elementary school years are crucial in a child's cognitive and affective development, and you are the central figure. You structure classroom experiences to implement the curriculum and create a supportive environment for learning to take place. In most activities, you are the guide, the coach, the facilitator, and the instigator of mathematical explorations.

- You give children the gift of self-confidence. Through your careful grouping, astute questions, appropriate tasks, and realistic expectations, each student can experience success.

- Long after they forget childhood events, your students will remember you. Your excitement and interest permeate the room and stimulate their appreciation for mathematics.

- Through your classroom practices, you promote mathematical thinking, reasoning, and understanding.

- You lay the foundation on which further study takes place. You give students multiple strategies and tools to solve problems. The questions you ask and the problems you pose can capture your students' imagination, arouse their curiosity, and encourage their creativity.

- You facilitate the building of their knowledge by giving them interesting problems to solve, which leads to the development of concepts and important mathematical ideas.

- Rules, algorithms, and formulas emerge from student explorations guided by you, the teacher of mathematics.

—Miriam A. Leiva, Curriculum and Evaluation Standards for School Mathematics, Addenda Series

Mathematics

In second grade students are beginning to recognize and use abstractions, and beginning to see the connection between the mathematical activities they perform and mathematical concepts. "Knowing" mathematics is "doing" mathematics. To learn and understand math concepts, students need to actively investigate mathematical concepts using many different materials. They must continually experience mathematics as a fundamental and important part of daily life, and develop awareness that mathematics is a foundation discipline for other disciplines. They also learn that mathematics is growing and changing.

Concepts

- The digits in the numeral denote how many ones, tens, hundreds, and so on, are in the number.

- Addition often requires carrying and regrouping into the next higher power of ten.

- Subtraction often requires borrowing, and regrouping into the next lower power of ten.

- Multiplication can be viewed as repeated addition.

- The unit fraction $1/n$ represents one of n equal-sized pieces of a whole.

- Addition and multiplication are commutative.

- Students recognize patterns and predict what will most likely come next. In second grade they begin to make connections between pictorial patterns and numerical patterns.

- Students continue to develop number sense—understanding the relationship of numbers to each other. They are able to tell when an answer or a unit of measurement is reasonable, and can use numbers effectively in many situations.

- Students measure quantities with appropriate units.

- Students collect, represent, analyze data, and make predictions about outcomes.

- Students analyze the properties of geometric figures and sort and classify geometric figures in many different ways.

Multicultural Education

Multicultural education is an interdisciplinary subject that should be a part of the everyday curriculum. The concepts can be included in any lesson that you present. The goal is to help students develop positive attitudes about themselves and other cultures. Through an anti-biased curriculum the students will learn to appreciate, respect, and value differences.

Concepts

- Each of us is a unique combination of family, preferences, dreams, abilities, emotions, and cultural background.

- Our country is made up of many cultures. Culture is a way of living shared by people in a group. Each culture represented in our country contributes to the society.

- Each person has dignity and worth. All have feelings that we can learn to recognize. Recognizing the feelings of others and reacting to them in positive ways can reduce conflict and create peace.

Curricular activities should build each student's intellectual and interpersonal skills. These activities should include defining oneself as a member of different kinds of groups, showing positive gender roles, and developing a cultural identity. The students should identify similarities and differences in different cultural groups, learn the achievements of people of diverse cultural groups that have made a difference to others, listen to others, and share their own feelings. Correct terminology should be used to identify various racial and ethnic groups. Above all, respect should be shown for all cultures.

Physical Education

In second grade students increase their strength and endurance, and improve their coordination and agility. There should also be a corresponding increase in the understanding and appreciation of fitness and its relation to physical activity.

Concepts

- Movement involves both small and large muscles. To perfect motor skills we all need repetitive practice. Movement can be coordinated into rhythmic patterns.

- Physical fitness concepts include learning that muscle strength can be increased by the use of progressive exercise. Cardiorespiratory endurance is important and can be increased by jogging or other similar exercise. Understanding the principles of exercise, cleanliness, and illness prevention is important.

- Self-knowledge can be developed by learning the importance of setting goals and working to achieve them. The difference between static and dynamic balance is understood.

- Social development through physical education includes several important concepts. Constructive comments from others are cues for improvement. Encouragement and praise should be extended to others. Borrowing equipment is a responsibility.

- Recreation is an important part of our lives, as is learning activities to use during leisure hours.

5

Science and Health

Science Concepts

Most state education standards and frameworks are based on the National Science Education Standards (NSES). The NSES presents its content standards by grade ranges, K-4, 5-8, and 9-12. Consequently, specific second-grade science study topics vary considerably from state to state and district to district. The NSES K-4 content standards published in 1996 follow. The science curriculum of your school or district will most likely reflect these content standards.

Unifying Concepts and Processes
- Systems, order, and organization
- Evidence, models, and explanation
- Change, constancy, and measurement
- Evolution and equilibrium
- Form and function

Science as Inquiry
- Abilities necessary to do scientific inquiry
- Understanding about scientific inquiry

Physical Science
- Properties of objects and materials
- Position and motion of objects
- Light, heat, electricity, and magnetism

Life Science
- Characteristics of organisms
- Life cycles of organisms
- Organisms and environments

Earth and Space Science
- Properties of earth materials
- Objects in the sky
- Changes in the earth and sky

Science and Technology
- Abilities to distinguish between natural objects and objects made by humans
- Abilities of technological design
- Understanding about science and technology

Science in Personal and Social Perspective
- Personal health
- Characteristics and changes in populations
- Types of resources
- Changes in environments
- Science and technology in local challenges

History and Nature of Science
- Science as a human endeavor

> **Learning science is something that students do, not something that is done to them. "Hands-on" activities are not enough. Students must have "minds-on" experience as well.**
>
> **—National Science Education Standards, 1996**

Sample Curriculum

Second graders make observations and conduct experiments which furnish information needed to progress from concrete operations to higher levels of abstraction. Students identify the ways that living organisms are dependent on one another and have adaptations that make it possible to survive in their particular environments. Students investigate various forms of energy and the relationship of matter and energy involving change of state, from a solid, liquid, and gas. Students explore the interaction of light and sound with different materials. Through diagrams and models, students deal with more abstract concepts about the relationship of the sun and earth to weather phenomena and seasons. Below you will find a sample curriculum that reflects topics frequently presented in second grade.

Physical Science

- Matter exists as solid, liquid, and gas. It changes state with the addition or loss of heat.

- Energy is necessary to do work or cause changes in matter; any kind of change requires energy.

- Objects containing iron can be magnetized; magnetism can be transferred to objects containing iron.

- Magnets have two poles; opposite poles attract and like poles repel each other. Magnetic force operates through some materials and over a distance.

- Light comes from a variety of sources and has characteristics by which it can be described. Very hot objects radiate light as well as heat.

- Light travels in a straight line; some materials can block or reflect light.

- Heat is essential for living things. Too much or too little heat can cause damage.

- Temperature is a measure of heat.

- Vibrating objects produce sound; sounds cause vibration in different materials, including the eardrum.

- Sound comes from many sources; sounds can travel through or be reflected or absorbed by various materials.

Life Science

- Organisms can be classified by similarities and differences.

- Plants have major structures with specific functions.

- Each kind of living organism has special needs, and has adapted to live in a habitat. It shares its environment with other living organisms to form communities.

- Fossil remains indicate that many species have become extinct and new species have come into being. Living things change with time.

Earth Science

- The earth rotates on its axis, a motion that causes the succession of night and day. The sun and moon appear to move across the sky.

- The moon is a natural satellite of the Earth and reflects light from the sun.

- Weather phenomena affect living organisms.

- The oceans, which cover about three-quarters of the earth's surface with salty water, are the major contributor to the water cycle and produce many natural resources.

- The earth's surface, including the ocean bottom, has a variety of topographical features which are changed over time by nature and by the activities of human beings.

- Rocks have characteristics by which they can be described and classified. Soils are formed from rocks.

- Earthquakes occur when parts of the earth move. Volcanic eruptions occur when magma is forced through openings in the earth's crust.

- Safety precautions taken in advance can reduce injury to people and damage to property when natural disasters occur.

Health

Health concepts and skills can be studied as part of your language arts, math, science, and arts programs, as well as a separate unit of study.

Concepts

- Personal good health is desirable. A balanced combination of physical activities, rest, recreation, and adequate diet contributes to fitness and cardiovascular health.

- Daily food intake affects our personal health.

- Understanding oneself and getting along with others is essential to good mental health. Understanding and coping with emotions in an acceptable way is healthy, while unresolved conflicts cause stress and anxiety which are unhealthy.

- Some substances may be beneficial when used properly, but can disrupt normal body functions when misused. Drugs are substances that change the way the mind and body work. We can be pressured by the environment or by those around us to use substances, but the choice to misuse them remains our own.

- Many factors contribute to diseases and disorders. How much we can control and prevent disease varies.

- Individuals are responsible for their own health and for knowing when to seek help from others. The community provides health-care resources. There are many careers in the field of health. A relationship exists between the quality of the environment and human health. We must all work to create and maintain a safe and healthful environment.

- Many accidents can be prevented. Each of us needs to be prepared to act effectively in times of emergency, including life-threatening situations. Safety can help reduce accidents and save lives.

Social Studies

The goal of a balanced elementary social studies program is to prepare students to participate in society with the knowledge, skills, and civic values that allow them to be actively and constructively involved. Second-grade students learn about people who make a difference in their lives. Beginning with a study of the family, including their grandparents and other ancestors, they construct simple family histories, and through them study the greater community, celebrating the achievements and contributions of historical figures. Many social studies concepts and skills can be studied as part of your language arts, math, science, and arts programs, as well as a separate unit of study.

Concepts

- People of the past influence our lives today.

- All people matter.

- People from all ethnic groups have and continue to contribute to our society.

- Physical features of land can be represented on map. Geography affects the quality and abundance of food we eat.

- People get what they need and want in exchange for what they have.

- We have a national identity, and constitutional and democratic heritages that have been defined by people from diverse cultural backgrounds working together.

Technology

Technology can be broadly divided into two areas. One is Industrial Technology—learning construction processes and skills using wood, paper, cardboard, and plastic, and the other is Computer Technology—learning fundamental computer concepts and tools. Curriculum development in this area is changing as fast as computer technology is. Many states and school districts are developing their academic standards in this field as this book goes to press. Check with your school or district.

Concepts

- Development and implementation of projects use problem-solving skills.

- Technology has components and processes.

- A systematic approach is a process.

Visual Arts and Music

Visual Arts

Second graders usually show perceptible growth in their abilities to represent form, space, and color. Their interest spans increase and they are aware of their environment. In second grade students are expected to master the concepts and skills that were previously introduced in kindergarten and developed in first grade.

Concepts

- The world can be perceived and described with images and symbols with visual and tactile qualities.

- Originality and personal experience are important to visual expression. Visual arts media can be used to communicate feelings and ideas.

- Art has played an important role in every culture throughout history. Studying art can give us insight into other people's lives.

- Using objective criteria for analysis, interpretation, and judgment based on aesthetic values results in informed responses to art and improved art production.

Music

In second grade students build upon previous musical activities with a variety of individual and large group activities. Students should sing and play short musical passages independently, express simple emotions with music and sing a variety of songs from around the world. They begin to differentiate between various musical elements and to create their own melodies and rhythms. Playing instruments and similar projects allows students to explore musical notation.

Concepts

- Rhythm flows on a recurring steady beat. It is divided into sets of accented and unaccented beats. The rhythm of the melody consists of longer and shorter sounds and silences. Meter is the organization of beats into groups of twos or threes.

- A melody is made up of tones with higher or lower pitches, that may change up or down or repeat. When a melody ends on the *home tone* a feeling of repose is created. Visual symbols can be used to show the relationships between tones. Tones in a melody may go up or down by a step (scale) or skip (chord).

- The basic form in music is the *phrase* or musical thought. Identical phrases contribute to the unity of a composition. A song or other composition may have an *introduction* or a *coda*. Contrasting phrases provide variety in compositions. Phrases may be partly the same or partly different.

- Songs can be performed with or without accompaniment. Harmony is created when two or more tones are sounded at the same time. Melodies may be combined resulting in a harmonic texture called polyphony. A musical composition may be either *major* or *minor* depending on its melody or harmony.

- Sound is produced in diverse ways and can be modified. Tempo is relative rather than absolute. Music can move in a fast or slow tempo. Dynamics in music can be louder or softer. Changes of tempo and dynamics provide a source of variety and expressive meaning in a composition. Characteristic qualities of sounds are determined by the types of voices or instruments which produce them.

- Music is a part of all cultures. It can be identified by characteristics. It has a cultural and historical context.

- Musical experience can be used to make intelligent judgments of musical value.

CHAPTER TWO: BRINGING THE CURRICULUM TO LIFE

LESSON PLANNING

Lesson planning is crucial to effectively organize your instruction. Some schools and districts require you to follow the teachers' manuals of commercially prepared textbook series. If your district does not require this, you will be responsible for planning your instructional year. There are as many ways to plan as there are teachers—so there is no one "right" way. The following is a guide.

Planning your program of instruction is like planning a dinner party. Before you begin to plan a dinner party, you know certain things. You know how many people you have invited and where you're going to hold the party. You have a certain time frame in mind, and you know that you are going to serve dinner.

First you must decide the presentation of your meal: will it be formal or informal? Sit-down dinner or buffet? Based on that decision you decide what the menu of your meal will be—something traditional or an ethnic meal? Do you want each food course to be completely different, or do you want the meal to have some unifying elements?

When you know the menu, you find the recipes, to review the ingredients and how to prepare them. You schedule your purchases and preparation time. Once the dinner is prepared you assess your results by tasting what you prepare, watching people eat the meal, and seeing what is left over.

Planning Steps

1. Review the curriculum.

2. Develop an overview of your program of instruction for the year—what concepts you will teach when (as a general idea).

3. Choose overarching themes that provide good frameworks for the concepts.

4. Decide what projects will promote the learning you want to see in the classroom within the theme and across the curriculum.

5. Choose activities to develop the skills that you want to focus on during the thematic unit.

6. Develop a calendar or time-line for the unit.

7. Create your weekly and daily plans.

Long-Term Planning

You can think of lesson planning in the same way as planning the dinner party. You know how many students you have, you know where you are going to teach them, and you know you are going to teach them the content and skills your school or district requires over the year. You will find this information in your school or district's curriculum guide or course of study. Ask your principal for a copy of the curricular requirements as soon as you can. You know that you need to organize all the information you must teach into a time frame—the school year.

Think about the concepts you want to teach over the next term. Decide what themes (the *presentation* of your school year) will provide good frameworks for these concepts. (Refer to the Using Themes section on page 16 for examples of themes.) Choose themes that will interest you and your students, and that are not too narrow in focus.

Decide what kinds of projects (the *menu*) will give your students many opportunities to learn and practice their learning. Projects can include anything from reading thirty pages in the textbook to converting your classroom into an imaginary rain forest.

Create, select, or choose activities (*recipes*) that will support the themes and promote the learning and practice of skills (*ingredients*).

Decide how many weeks (or days) you will need to accomplish your projects. Make a calendar or time-line of the unit.

Now that you know **what** you want to accomplish you need to plan **how** you will accomplish your long-term plans. Your weekly and daily lesson plans are the way to organize your activities into a feasible schedule.

A commercial lesson-plan book will be a useful purchase if your school or district does not provide one. There are many varieties from which to choose, from the most basic notebook-sized with gridded pages to large planbooks that include lesson plan ideas.

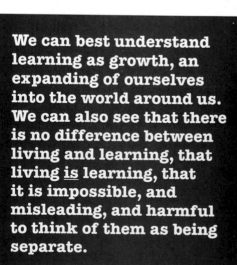

We can best understand learning as growth, an expanding of ourselves into the world around us. We can also see that there is no difference between living and learning, that living is learning, that it is impossible, and misleading, and harmful to think of them as being separate.

—John Holt, <u>What Do I Do Monday?</u>, 1970

Skills

- Alphabetize the names of animals and plants.
- Write. Keep a personal journal.
- Explore the concepts of volume and capacity.
- Collect, organize, display, interpret, and analyze data in concrete, pictorial, and bar graphs.
- Explore the relationships between addition/subtraction, multiplication/division.
- Play Football (team sport). Play Team ball with parachute.
- Use a variety of painting techniques.
- Organize objects of varying forms into a 3-dimensional arrangement.
- Explore and organize objects.
- Design simple investigations to test an hypothesis.
- Locate information by interviewing. Compare and contrast ideas about the same issue from different sources.

Projects

- Choral read poems – experiment with different rhythms.
- Design and paint murals based on the book.
- Make individual terrariums from soda bottles, stock some with insects. Experiment with overwatering and different soil types–observing results.
- Review what services are offered in the community using phone books.
- Walking tour of the neighborhood. Develop an action plan for how to improve the community.
- Create Fact Families.
- Visit local nursery or farm. Find out what food plants are grown locally. Survey what food is grown locally. Find out where the rest of it comes from.
- Survey local wildlife. Why does it live in our neighborhood?
- Make diorama of neighborhood

Theme

healthy communities

Concepts

Language Arts
- language as written communication
- group publication and choral reading

Mathematics
- number sense and fact families

Science
- Each kind of living organism has special needs, and has adapted to live in a habitat. It shares its environment with other living organisms to form communities.

Health
- A relationship exists between the quality of the environment and human health.

Social Studies
- Geography affects the quality and abundance of food we eat.
- People get what they need and want in exchange for what they have.

Literature Needed

Land, Sea, & Sky: Poems to Celebrate the Earth, Catherine Paladino (Little, Brown and Company, 1993); The Hidden Life of the Meadow by David M. Schwartz (Crown Publishers, 1988); Earth Child, Kathryn Sheehan and Mary Waidner (Council Oak Books, 1991); Getting to Know the World's Greatest Artists (Children's Press, 1988) need prints of murals by Diego Rivera, Chagall, and others

Materials Needed

tempera paint
paintbrushes
water containers
large sheets of paper
oak tag

empty soda bottles
soil
plants
seeds
insects
construction paper

Weekly Plans

Make detailed plans and schedule your instruction a week in advance. Include any regular or unusual events in the plan, such as school assemblies, class visitors, library visits, or short school days. Decide what lessons you want to include in the week and fit them into your schedule. The Scheduling section on page 70 will assist you in deciding when to teach what.

Daily Plans

For your daily plans you will want to balance activities that require sitting with activities where your students can move around. To begin the year you should assume that 20 minutes is long enough to require your students to stay focused on the same thing. As they grow, and you get to know them better, you will find what time frame works for your students. You will also discover exactly what a "wide range of abilities" means. Some students can do whatever you ask them to do, well, in less than half the time that other students require. Plan extension activities or extra projects that will engage these students when they have finished required work. In addition, as you are planning, you may want to decide what homework activities to assign.

Planning a Lesson

Decide what the focus or purpose of the lesson is. It should be clearly stated, because the clearer your purpose, the easier to design a lesson that accomplishes the purpose. Some examples of purposes follow.

- The purpose of this activity is to have students find many different addends that give the same sum.

- The purpose of this activity is to have students identify the main ideas of their favorite stories.

List the materials that will be needed. If you need to order any supplies or get other items, you can do so in advance.

Plan the introduction to your lesson to give students background knowledge that will help them understand the new information. Literature, songs, and pictures can build background knowledge and motivate your students.

Plan exactly what you are going to do and how you are going to do it. Walk through the procedure in your head. If the lesson involves following directions and/or making something, do the activity yourself before you present it to your class. This will help you identify trouble spots. It is much easier to make necessary adjustments before you present it to a group of excited second graders.

After you present the lesson your students should have time to work independently on the skill you have presented. This gives them the practice necessary to learn it. You may wish to have the students work on the skill in small groups.

Planning for Assessment

The final element to consider is how to assess the effectiveness of the lesson. Use informal observations of students involved in the independent activity planned for the lesson combined with formal checks of the work. For more information on assessment and record keeping, see pages 72 and 73.

Thinking through and planning each lesson is essential to your becoming the most effective teacher you can be.

Good teaching is one-fourth preparation and three-fourths theatre.

—Gail Godwin, <u>The Odd Woman</u>, 1974

Day _____ **Date** _____

Time	Project Description	Materials Needed	Special Materials or Instructions

Teacher: Make copies of this form to use in your daily planning. Fill in the information you need to organize your day.

USING THEMES

Themes are big ideas, larger than facts, concepts, and skills. Using a theme allows you to integrate several content areas into meaningful learning activities, then provides you with a framework to guide you in the design and development of your instructional program. A theme provides you a way to make words and abstract ideas concrete, and to help your students see how ideas relate to other ideas and to their own experiences.

Themes link concepts and skills for your students. As you present new lessons framed in the context of your thematic unit, students can easily add the new information to the knowledge they already have. It is easier for students to learn skills, because they have knowledge and experience which create a context within which to apply the skills.

Samples of Second-Grade Themes

Dinosaurs

As facets of the dinosaur theme, you and your students could read and write about dinosaurs (language arts), use dinosaur manipulatives in math activities, discuss and explore fossils and the environments in which dinosaurs lived (science), make dinosaur clay figures (visual arts), and draw a life-sized dinosaur outline on your playground based on measurements you find in an encyclopedia or dinosaur reference book (math, science, visual arts).

Shelter

As facets of the shelter theme you and your class could explore literature to learn about different kinds of houses people live in around the world (language arts), build models of different kinds of housing (visual arts and social studies), make a map of the houses where your students live (math, social studies), and discuss how weather and climate affect housing needs (science).

Light

Read poetry about light and dark. Read "Goodnight, Moon" by Margaret Wise Brown and make student versions of the book based on their rooms (language arts); make models of the moon orbiting around the Earth, build and use a solar oven to bake a cake (science and industrial technology); explore making shadows in a variety of situations such as using the overhead projector to project mystery objects onto the wall (math) or using the sun to make large and small shadows with bodies on the playground and measure the shadows at different times of the day (physical education and math); make sun photos by placing objects on dark construction paper and exposing them to strong sunlight without moving for several hours, explore photography (science and visual arts); explore prisms (science); compare how people live in areas where the length of day remains relatively constant throughout the year (near the equator) with how people live in areas nearer the poles like North America, Northern Europe, South Africa, or Australia (social studies); create silhouette pictures by projecting students' shadows onto paper and tracing around them, look at paintings by some of the French impressionist painters and discuss how light is used, and copy some of the paintings (visual arts).

LANGUAGE ARTS

As you plan your language arts program, remember that you can use reading and writing in all curricular areas for assessment purposes. Although language arts processes apply across the curriculum, some specific skills to address in second grade are listed below. They are not listed in any particular order.

- Respond appropriately to spoken, written, and nonverbal directions.

- Make predictions about stories.

- Combine simple sentences into complex statement, commands, and/or questions.

- Keep a personal journal.

- Alphabetize names, places, things, and other new vocabulary to the third letter.

- State personal reactions.

- Write stories of one or more paragraphs accompanied by appropriate titles, signs, captions, illustrations, posters, murals, or paper constructions such as pop-up cards or dioramas.

- Recognize and use correct syntax when editing personal and peer writing.

- Use synonyms and antonyms for words learned through reading.

- Edit own and peer writing by proofreading for:

  — conventional spelling of familiar words;

  — correct punctuation of sentences and common abbreviations used in street addresses, in contractions, and in quotations; and,

  — correct capitalization of proper nouns, words at the beginning of sentences, and for the first word in lines of rhymed poetry.

- State specific details that explain the main idea or theme found in pictures, plays, book covers, or text.

- Share favorite literary works and explain why they are personal favorites.

- Draw conclusions based on evidence found through reading.

- Distinguish between fact and opinion.

- Distinguish between real and unreal subjects found through reading.

- Use the tables of contents to locate information in books.

- Continue to develop legible handwriting.

- Phonics instruction includes short and long vowel sounds, consonant blends, consonant digraphs, two-letter regular vowels, vowel digraphs, controlled vowels, and diphthongs.

> **If we value independence, if we are disturbed by the growing conformity of knowledge, of values, of attitudes, which our present system induces, then we may wish to set up conditions of learning which make for uniqueness, for self-direction, and for self-initiated learning.**
>
> —Carl R. Rogers, <u>On Becoming a Person</u>, 1961

Reading

Most students enter second grade reading and writing. The range of their skills is wide; you will have some students who read and write well, some who are barely reading and writing, and those in-between. Generally second-grade students begin reading chapter books. They develop their abilities to recognize cause and effect, make story predictions, draw conclusions based on concrete evidence, data, or context clues, and distinguish between fact and opinion.

There are three important components to a good reading program: guided reading, shared oral reading, and independent reading. Many second-grade reading programs are implemented as Reading and Writing Workshops which combine the three important reading components, with a strong writing component.

Guided Reading

In guided reading you read with students. You can work with students individually or in groups. Guided reading allows you to listen to students as they read to closely monitor progress. The student could produce written and oral work related to what has been read in the guided-reading group. While guided-reading groups are meeting, other students in the class work on reading projects or work that you assign.

Shared Oral Reading

Every day spend time reading to your class. Shared oral reading can be used to introduce or support themes or new activities, provide background information, practice reading strategies, or just share the pleasure of reading. You could use a big book and read while the class follows along with you, read a book and have students follow along with you in copies of the book, or choose a favorite children's novel and read a chapter every day until you have finished it.

Independent Reading

D.E.A.R. Time

D.E.A.R. time means Drop Everything And Read time. Many schools recommend or require D.E.A.R. time. If yours doesn't, you may wish to implement it in your classroom. During D.E.A.R. time the only activity going on in your room is reading. Your students read, classroom visitors read, and you read.

Sustained Silent Reading (SSR)

During the Sustained Silent Reading period students read to themselves. Depending on your schedule and your students' abilities, you will want this period to last 10-30 minutes. The room should be quiet and the students encouraged to read books at their ability level for the duration of the SSR period. SSR can make an excellent entry task.

Buddy Reading

Two students sit side by side with a book crossing their laps. One student reads while the other student actively listens and coaches. When the reader gets stuck, the other student will ask, "Do you want think time or coaching?" When a student chooses think time, the reading buddy remains silent. This allows the student to think about his or her reading. If the student chooses coaching, the reading buddy offers help using a reading strategy. Model this process a few times before having students practice on their own. It may take time for students to catch on, but once they do, you will find them buddy-reading during their spare time.

Phonics

Your school or district may require you to use a formal phonics program. If not, recognize that phonics instruction is one tool to use when teaching reading. Demonstrate letter sounds to your students while you are working in guided reading groups. Use words that are part of their reading to present the sounds that are causing your students difficulty.

Phonics instruction includes the short vowels, long vowels, consonant blends, consonant digraphs, two-letter regular vowels, vowel digraphs, controlled vowels, and diphthong.

Writing

Writing is an essential part of language arts learning. Research has proven that writing improves reading.

TIP!

Post student names on a class chart in alphabetical order. Use the chart as a reference for starting sounds, vowels, and blends.

Interactive Writing

Identify a skill you want students to work on and develop a writing topic or specific sentences that you want them to write. Set up an easel, chart paper, markers, correction tape and a pointer in your group area. Call on a student to choose an assistant. The two of them will write the words you dictate on the chart—one writing and the other making hand and finger spaces to create the correct spacing for paragraphs and words in a sentence. Engage the remaining students in clapping the syllables, finding rhyming words to the word that is being spelled, or standing for uppercase letters and squatting for lower case letters. Great subjects for this writing technique are field trips, new math procedures, and writing word problems. The key is to read the written material aloud to reinforce the concepts with the students. This activity should be done in approximately 20 minutes or less.

Reading Strategies

1. Try that word again.
2. Take a running start. (Start reading the entire sentence again from the beginning.)
3. Look at the picture cues.
4. Get your mouth ready.
5. Break the word into parts.
6. Ask a friend.

19

Writer's Workshop

Writing workshops give your students a great deal of practice in all phases of the writing process. A great advantage of a writing workshop is that the students can work at their own paces. The students start the year as beginning writers and develop and sharpen their writing skills over the year. They look forward to writing time when they can be creative, productive, and challenged all at the same time.

Organizing Student Papers

You need designated spots where students keep their works-in-progress. You will want to have bins or trays for each stage of the writing process, labeled as Prewriting; Rough Drafts; Revisions; Proofs; Waiting for Publication; and Published Not Presented. It is easy for students to find their projects and for you to review the products in process.

Writing and Art Supplies

Create a supply area of materials for students to use for illustrations and shaped papers or paper templates for students to use for final copies.

Electronic Publishing

It is extremely helpful to have a parent volunteer assist with the Workshop. If you have a computer in your classroom, or a volunteer who will do word processing for you, student books could be electronically published. Electronic publishing adds an exciting touch to the process for your students.

Mini-lessons

A mini-lesson should only last five to ten minutes and be focused on a specific topic. The mini-lessons can be used across the curriculum to introduce centers, new procedures, or new materials. As you review the works-in-progress you will identify areas you want your students to strengthen. Students may also suggest topics to you. Some topics you could cover are listed below.

- Expectations and classroom management

- Brainstorming

- How to use writing workshop bins and writing and art materials

- How you want students to set up their papers

- How to help each other

- The writing process

- Your expectations about spacing between letters and words on handwritten work

- Punctuation

- Spelling and proofreading

- How to choose a writing topic

- Different genres

- Characters and Setting

- Conflict/Solution

You can include anything in the mini-lesson you think is appropriate and present it to the whole class or only to a few who may need it.

Status Checks

Ask each student, "What will you be working on?" The student could reply, "I'm rewriting my story," or "I'm editing my draft," or "I'm working on the illustrations for my book." The status check should only take two to three minutes. Based on the responses you receive, you know who needs help right away.

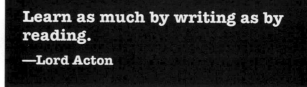

Learn as much by writing as by reading.

—Lord Acton

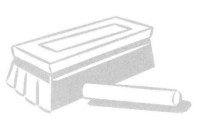

Individual Writing Conferences

As you meet with a student or students during this 20- to 25-minute time period, the others are writing. During the writing conference, follow these guidelines.

- Listen to the student.

- Respond to the content of the writing first.

- Follow the student as he or she reads the work.

- Work on one problem at a time.

- Keep the conference short.

Revision

There are several ways to handle the revision process. One way is to have all the revision interaction centered around you. You meet with the student, make comments and suggestions, and then he or she revises based on your comments. Another way is to have your students present their work in progress to several other students individually or at the same time. Constructive comments are used to assist in the revision process by the author-presenter. A combination of these two methods may work best for you.

Author's Chair

Designate an Author's Chair. At the end of the Writer's Workshop session, students share their works with the other students in the class as well as with the teacher. Encourage students to make positive comments to the author about his or her work. Your students will shine with pride.

Local Authors in the Classroom Library

Regularly have students contribute their work to a special section for "local authors" of your classroom library. You may wish to protect the original work by laminating it or making copies for students to peruse.

The Writing Process

- Prewriting—getting ideas on paper

- Drafting—rough draft stage

- Revising—reviewing and changing work

- Proofreading—correcting spelling, syntax, and mechanical errors

- Publishing—creating the final copy

- Sharing—presenting the work

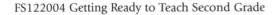

Frequently Used Words

a	her	people
after	here	play
all	him	put
am	his	run
an	house	ran
and	how	said
are	I	saw
as	I'm	see
asked	if	she
at	in	so
away	into	some
back	is	that
be	it	the
because	just	then
before	keep	there
big	kind	they
boy	know	this
but	like	three
by	little	to
came	look	too
can	looked	two
come	long	up
could	make	us
day	man	very
did	mother	was
do	me	we
don't	my	went
down	no	were
for	not	what
from	now	when
get	of	where
go	old	will
going	on	with
good	one	would
had	or	you
has	our	your
have	out	
he	over	

> **Learning is a developmental process that takes time and is often hard work.**
>
> —National Science Education Standards, 1996

Spelling Strategies

Your school district may have a formal spelling program to follow. If not, you will want to develop lists of words for your students to learn based on what they are reading or difficulties they are having in their writing. Encourage students to use spelling strategies and invented spelling while they are writing. As part of the editing process, teach students to look at the word and ask, "What looks right?" Encourage students to use the word wall and their personal dictionaries to become independent spellers.

Personal Dictionaries

Students make personal dictionaries to use as a tool when writing. The pages should be arranged in alphabetical order with the letter of the alphabet placed at the top of the page, like a printed dictionary. You can preprint the pages on a photocopier with the high frequency words included already. When a student asks for the spelling of a word, he or she records the correct spelling in the personal dictionary. From that point on, the student can look up the word as it is used.

Frequently Used Words

Frequently used words appear over and over in stories. It is useful for students to know these word to increase their reading and writing fluency. Sight words can also be used to figure out unfamiliar words.

Word Wall

Post the alphabet on a wall or a bulletin board. Include upper case and lower case forms of each letter (letter grouping). Leave enough space so that you can create a column of words beneath each letter grouping. Review frequently-used words with the class and/or words they commonly spell incorrectly. Students build the word wall with your assistance throughout the year, placing each word in alphabetical order under the correct letter of the alphabet. They can use the word wall as a reference when they don't know how to spell a word.

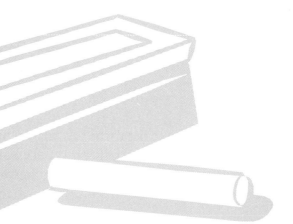

Language Arts Activities

Morning Message

Start each day with a written morning message addressed to the class. Write it on the chalkboard before students enter the classroom and read during group time.

Word of the Day

One way to expand your students' vocabularies is to focus on a word of the day. Prepare word and definition strips in advance. Write the words with their definitions on index cards. Put them in a box. Have one student choose a word. Write the word on the board and go over the definition. Ask the class to come up with a synonym and an antonym. As you move through the school year, have students choose the word of the day. They use the dictionary as a reference, write the word and definition, and present the word to the class. The word cards can be filed alphabetically and kept in the area of the classroom where you keep your dictionaries.

> **TIP!**
>
> *Some authors and poets appropriate for second grade include Robert Munch, Dr. Seuss, Mercer Meyer, Tomie de Paola, Jane Yolen, and Jack Prelutsky.*

Label the Room

Use interactive writing to label objects in the classroom to develop vocabulary and spelling resources. (A presentation of interactive writing is found on page 19.) Choose objects in the room to label. As students take turns writing the words help them with the correct spelling if necessary. Go one step further and add a second language to the label by using a foreign language-English dictionary

English	window
Spanish	la ventana
French	la fenêtre

Quick Comments

This is a quick way to check reading or listening comprehension and provide a forum for students to express their opinions about a book read in class. Ask each student what he or she thought about the book. The students can either comment or pass.

Author Study

Choose an author of books for children who has published at least four different books. Make sure to have multiple copies of the titles selected. Explore the author's style as a class through question and answer discussions. Then focus on one story element per day, such as story structure (beginning, middle, or end), setting, characters, or conflict and resolution. Provide students with half sheets of paper on which they write the title of the book, the author, and the story element discussed. Students decorate their papers with borders or illustrations inspired by the book. Display the work.

Poetry

Poems should be a part of everyday school life. They are easy to use because frequently they are short in length and are fun to do as choral reading. Introduce at least two poems a week. You can distribute copies of poems or have students copy them from the board or a posterboard. Have students illustrate each poem after it is read aloud and discussed, and store their copies in a poetry folder. Specific skills can be easily demonstrated through the use of poetry. These skills include punctuation, spelling, rhyming words, and patterns. Regularly reread favorite poems.

Four Corners

Post four different genre names in different sections of the room. Begin with the genres of non-fiction, fiction, mystery, and fantasy. Review the characteristics of the different types of books. Students choose their favorite types of books and go to the designated area where they talk about why they like to read that particular type of book. They can list the titles of their favorite books on large pieces of paper. This activity can be adapted and used for other class discussions based on topics like movies, school subjects, recess activities, and so on. You can extend this activity across the curriculum by taking the quantitative results (5 students like nonfiction, 4 like fiction, 8 students like mysteries, and 3 like fantasy) and turning them into a simple bar graph.

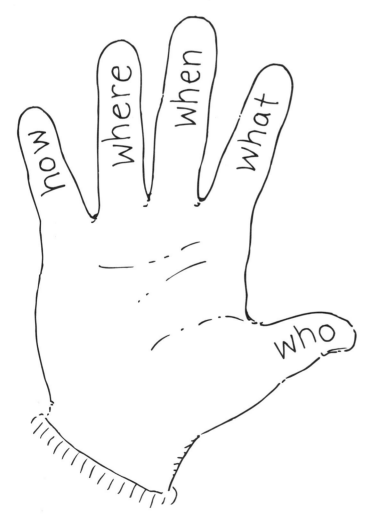

> **The object of education is to prepare the young to educate themselves throughout their lives.**
> —Robert Hutchins

On-hand Checking

Students use their hands as graphic organizers to check their writings. The student examines his or her writing to see *who* did *what* and *when* it was done. He or she will also check for *why* and *where* the event took place. Invent a cue phrase to remind your students to use their portable checking tool.

The Play's the Thing

After reading a story with the class, divide the students into groups of four or five. Each group writes a play based on the story. First they pick which characters and settings they will include and decide whether to use a narrator. Then they write the dialogue. Changing scenes and any important actions that move the plot forward are written as stage directions to the actors. The students will enjoy using their creativity and moving around as they work together. This project could also be accomplished as puppet theater. You will want to schedule this project over a period of several days.

Journals

There are many uses for journals in the classroom. They can range from daily journals with entry tasks, to science and math journals, to free response journals. Reading journals can be used in which students record the titles and authors of the books they have read, and any comments about the book. Journals are a great way to involve students in writing. End the day with a reflection journal in which each student writes about his or her day. Students could also write to you. Every day after you review the journals, you can respond to their comments, or write personal notes of encouragement to them.

Types of Sentences

Prepare sentence strips illustrating different types of sentences without including the end punctuation. Create enough sentence strips so that when you group your students, each group will have three or four sentences. You could use sentences from the literature that the class is reading. Model three types of sentences—statements, questions, and exclamations. Ask your students to analyze the sentences using the question, "Does this sentence tell information, ask information, or exclaim something?"

Divide your students into groups of three or four. Give each group three or four sentence strips to identify. Have one student in the group read a sentence to the class and identify the ending mark. Make sure the class agrees and can justify why that ending mark was used. Discuss alternative possibilities such as a sentence that can end with a period or an exclamation mark. An example of this kind of sentence is *They arrived home* which can be punctuated, *They arrived home.* or *They arrived home!*

Compound Words

Compound words are made up of two words. Write compound words on note cards. Cut each card to separate the two words. Students can work together to reform the compound words. Give each student a card and have her or him draw a picture illustrating the word. Instruct students to find the owner of the word card needed to complete a compound word. Tape the two cards together. Have partners work together to draw a picture of the compound word. Review the words and artwork as a class. Place the cards at the writing center for reference.

Letter Writing Center

Students enjoy writing letters to classmates, teachers, or family members. After discussing proper letter formats in a lesson, post the correct letter format for students to follow. Students will also enjoy writing letters to their favorite authors.

Pen-Pals

Have students write letters to real pen-pals. The pen-pals could be at your school or a different school. Exchange letters with a teacher from another school, investigate pen-pal organizations for students on the Internet, or use international pen-pal organizations found through children's magazines. Use good sense about your pen-pal source. Use a legitimate organization that screens participating groups to verify they are children. Students could exchange pictures with the letters and get together at the end of the year if geographically feasible.

Spelling Baseball

Prepare four lists of spelling words—one of easy words, the second of grade-level words, the third of difficult words, and the fourth of challenging words. Divide the students into two teams. Label different parts of the room first base, second base, third base, and home plate to simulate a baseball diamond. Students take turns going "to bat." Each student decides if he or she wants to try for a single, double, triple hit, or a home run. You select an appropriate word for the "batter" to spell. If the "batter" correctly spells the word, he or she walks around the bases to the correct one. When a "batter" cannot spell the word, a person on base can steal a base if he or she can spell that word. Each player who crosses home plate earns a point for his or her team. The "three-strikes-and-you're-out" rule applies here. When three students are out, the teams trade places.

Q: What kind of license does a refrigerator have?

A: A license to chill.

Q: What kinds of keys don't open doors?

A: Monkeys and donkeys.

Q: What do you call a funny snake?

A: Hiss-terical.

Building Words

Choose a long word like *hippopotamus*. Make a list of other words that can be made from the letters of this word. Choose 12 to 15 words from your list that will reinforce patterns, little words in big words (like *hip*), or words that can be made with the same letters in different places (*tops* and *stop*). Write all the words on index cards and put them in order from smallest to biggest. Put the cards in an envelope and label the outside with the words for your lesson. Provide each student with the word *hippopotamus* cut into separate letters. Direct students how to make the words using the letters. One student from the class can make the words in a pocket chart at the front of the class while the other students build the words at their desks.

Make a Commercial

Divide the class into groups of four or five. Each group creates a three-minute commercial featuring one favorite book that all the group members have read. The commercials should include: a commentary; a mention of the important characters in the book; how the author made the story special; and why the students would recommend the books. Using a video or a tape recorder, the students record the commercial. If you do not have access to a video or tape recorder, students can present their commercials live and in person!

Hot Seat

Introduce character traits, check for comprehension, and reinforce elements of a story by assigning one student to become a character from a book. The student in character sits facing the other students. Students take turns asking the character questions, who answers them "in character."

Tongue Twisters

Students practice writing and spelling, and twist their tongues around the following tongue twisters to work on blends and phonemic awareness. Create a student-printed and -illustrated tongue twister book for the class library. Include some original tongue twisters written by your students.

Claire's class clapped for the clumsy clown.

Drew dreamed dreadful dragons dropped Drew's drum.

Grouchy Grace grows green grapes.

Sleepy Slick slipped on a slimy, slippery sled.

Tracy transformed triple transformers into trains and trucks.

Monthly Laughathon

Second graders have great senses of humor. Once a month, have students share their favorite jokes and riddles with the class. Then have students write and illustrate their jokes and riddles to compile into a class book for the classroom library.

Name: _____ **Date:** _____

Organizing My Ideas

Directions: Use the table below to help organize your thoughts. First pick something that you want to write about. Write it in on the top of the table. You need to give the table some legs so that it doesn't fall over, so write four sentences to support your idea—one on each table leg. Write a concluding sentence on the floor.

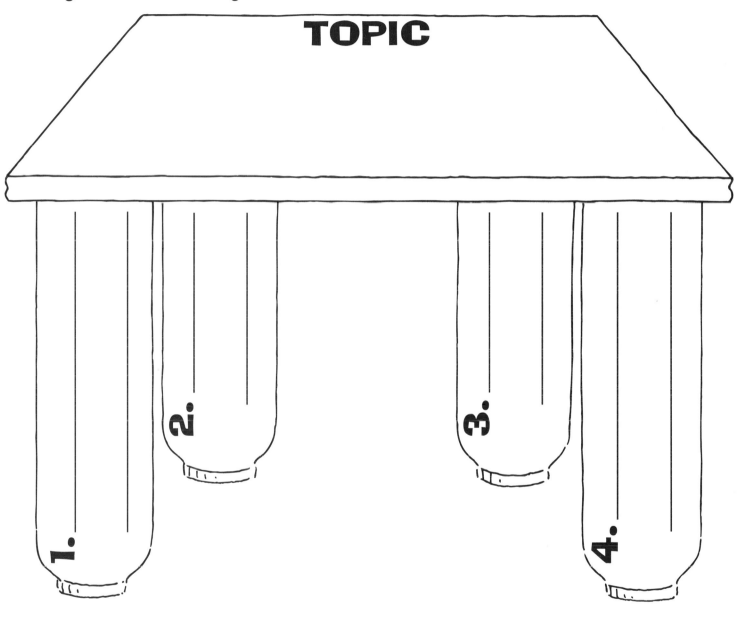

CONCLUSION: _____

_____

_____

Use your graphic organizer to write a paragraph on the back of this paper. Remember to start with a topic sentence.

MATHEMATICS

Skills

- Classify objects using shape, size, or other attributes.

- Classify objects and record results using two or more attributes.

- Construct and describe the properties of the following geometric shapes: circle, square, triangle, and rectangle. Relate these shapes to the environment.

- Find lines of symmetry in geometric shapes and in the environment.

- Estimate and measure length in nonstandard, customary, and metric units.

- Estimate and measure area in nonstandard units.

- Estimate and measure volume and capacity in nonstandard, customary, and metric units.

- Read time on both digital and analog clocks. Increments students should be able to identify and use are the hour, the half hour, the quarter hour, and five-minute intervals.

- Use a calendar to read and locate days, weeks, months, year, and significant events.

- Compare equivalent combinations of coins totaling one dollar.

- Make change for one dollar.

- Recognize and extend patterns.

- Express an ordered pair for a specific point on a number plane.

- Graph the ordered pair for a function.

- Collect, organize, display, interpret, and analyze data in concrete, pictorial, and bar graphs.

- Predict outcomes and record results of simple probability experiments.

- Identify the operation symbol needed to make a number sentence true (+, -, =, <, >, x, ÷)

- Count by twos, fives, and tens.

- Count backward from a given number.

- Count groups of ten objects as though they were single groups.

- Express numbers in standard and expanded notation to express quantities of objects.

- Round to the nearest ten.

- Examine the properties of even and odd numbers. Explore which numbers can be evenly divided into two equal groups.

- Express a number that comes before or after a given number, or between two given numbers.

- Compare and order numbers through hundreds by using logic and reason.

- Use problem-solving strategies to demonstrate understanding of addition and subtraction.

- Solve problems that require addition and subtraction, including money.

- Use estimation and mental arithmetic strategies to find sums or differences of numbers.

- Explore the concepts of multiplication and division by grouping objects and examining patterns.

- Explore the relationship between multiplication and division facts.

- Illustrate and describe the fractional parts of a whole object using terms such as one-half, one-third, and one-fourth.

- Addition and subtraction facts for numbers 1 to 9.

- Read numbers to 1,000.

Math Activities

Math Center

Provide an area of math exploration, discovery, and practice with a math center. The center should include a variety of manipulatives stored in tubs. These could include a variety of counters, buttons, linking cubes, pattern blocks, calculators, play money, and several classroom manipulative clocks. The students use the manipulatives to practice classification, addition and subtraction, multiplication and division, explore symmetry, tell time, count money, and to create patterns.

Math Stumper

During math time, write a challenging problem on the board. When students finish their assignments, they try to solve the stumper. Make it challenging enough to require them to think and use problem-solving skills.

Sample Stumper:

Cameron used 2 pounds of flour to make his famous chocolate cake for 8 people. How many pounds of flour would he need to make chocolate cake for 24 people?

Skip Counting

Warm up the class at the beginning of math time by having students skip count by twos, fives, and tens. Have the students count backwards by skip counting as well.

Number Chart

Use a wall number chart of numbers 1 to 100 to practice skip counting patterns of twos, fives, and tens. Introduce skip counting by threes, fours, eights, and nines using the chart. If your chart is laminated, you can write on it with a non-permanent marker to indicate which numbers will be counted in the skip-counting pattern you have chosen. See if your students notice any visual patterns to the skip counting.

For the following activities, make multiple copies of the Number Chart worksheet on page 39 for each student.

Use the Number Chart 1–100 to guide students to find all the numbers that end in zero, three, or one. What patterns do the students recognize?

Guide students to explore skip-counting patterns. The students will begin to recognize other patterns independently. As their thinking develops, students can follow other patterns using numbers. One activity would be to color every third number (3, 6, 9, 12, and so on) and have students practice skip counting by threes. What do they notice about the pattern?

Hand out copies of the Number Chart 1–100 with missing numbers (white out some of the squares before you photocopy it). Have students fill in the missing numbers. Discuss the ways they can figure out the missing numbers such as counting, looking at visual patterns on the chart, or comparing it to a complete hundred chart.

As their number sense develops you can cut the complete Number Chart 1–100 into sections like puzzle pieces. Have students put the puzzle together. Give them charts to make their own puzzles. An extension of this activity is to use the Number Chart 1–100 with blanked numbers. Cut the chart into puzzle pieces for students to assemble. They will have to complete number patterns to assemble the puzzle correctly. Eventually you will be able to provide a jigsaw piece of the chart with only one number on it, and your students will be able to complete the missing numbers correctly.

Number Line

Post a number line around your room. Use it to count backward and forward from different starting numbers, for skip counting, and to demonstrate addition and subtraction problems.

Counting Back and Forth

Pick a number where you want students to start counting. Tell them whether to count forward or backward in their heads while they clap out loud. Stop after a certain number of claps and ask a student what the number is. For example, starting with 156, clap six times, and have students give you the ending number (162).

Even and Odd Counting Activities

Assign each student a number. Call each number asking the students to form an *odds* line and an *evens* line.

When counting in class, have students stand on odd numbers and sit on even numbers.

Students can use their hands to help them remember the concept of odd and even numbers. Have students make fists of their hands, and then extend one finger on one hand. Direct them to extend the matching finger on the other hand. The fingers with partners are even, the fingers that do not have partners are odd. Continue to count with the students until all ten fingers are extended, saying odd or even as appropriate. Announce different numbers between one and ten and have students identify them odd or even and test the answer.

Time

Use a clock manipulative such as a Judy clock to teach time. It is extremely useful to have small versions of the clock faces that the students can manipulate.

Set up your room so that students develop and practice their time-telling skills as they figure out when things are happening throughout their days. Daily practice reading clocks makes learning how to tell time easier.

Include a clock graphic that shows the time an activity begins on your daily schedule. If a student asks, "When is recess?", refer him or her to the schedule and a manipulative clock and demonstrate how to figure out how much time until recess. When students know how to figure out the answer, they can answer their own time questions independently by apply their knowledge to different situations. Using a clock during morning opening time also reinforces these skills.

Make time flashcards, with the hour, minute and a.m. or p.m. on them. Put the cards in a pocket chart and have a student draw three cards. The student displays the cards and states the time. As the student is showing the time on the clock, ask the rest of the class, "What time will it be in two hours? One hour before? or, 15 minutes later?"

Stamps with clock dials are available in teacher supply stores. They are useful for communicating times on notes to parents and students.

Reading digital-time clocks should be practiced as well.

Reversibility

Reversibility in math is known as the commutative property. Teach students that the order of the numbers in an addition or multiplication math equation does not affect the answer. For example, 1 + 6 is the same as 6 + 1. Students explore this information by making a model. Have students choose an equation to reverse. They fold a piece of construction paper in half and write the equation on one half of the paper, and the reverse on the other half. Using beans or shells to represent the numbers, the student glues the correct quantities on each half of the paper to verify that both equations have the same answer.

Fact Family

It is important that students know how number facts are related to one another. Write an addition fact. Rewrite the addition fact exchanging the locations of the addends. Then write the subtraction equations that are part of the same fact family. After presenting several similar models see whether your students recognize any patterns in the fact families. For example look at the fact family for the number 9.

8 + 1 = 9	1 + 8 = 9
9 - 8 = 1	9 - 1 = 8

Solving Equations Using Algebra

Have students find the missing numbers in equations like the ones listed below. Students can create their own problems and exchange them with a friend to solve.

5 + ? = 8   ? + 3 = 9   10 + ? = 20

Problem of the Day

During opening activities, have students come up with the "problem of the day." Students create a math equation that equals the number value of the date. For example, if the date is the October 25, a possible problem would be 20 + 5 = 25. The students enjoy making up problems. Encourage them to create double digit addition and subtraction problems such as, 13 + 12= 25 or 100 − 75 = 25.

"I wonder why . . .?"

"What would happen if . . .?"

"Tell me about your pattern."

"Can you do it another way?"

"Our group has a different solution."

These inviting words give students the freedom to be creative, the confidence to solve problems, and the power to do mathematics. When you give your students the opportunity to construct their own knowledge, you are opening the doors of mathematics to all young learners.

This is the challenge. This is the vision.

—Miriam A. Leiva, <u>Curriculum and Evaluation Standards for School Mathematics, Addenda Series</u>

Math Relays

Practice math facts with a relay race. Place addition and subtraction flash cards in a box. Divide the class into two teams. One player from each team draws a flash card. They both race to the chalkboard by walking backwards, hopping, jogging, or skipping where they write the problem and the correct answer. The team with the most correct answers wins.

31

Symbols

It is important that students know the symbols for less than (<), greater than (>), and equal to (=), to deepen their understanding of number sense as well as improve their ability to solve equations. Young students often get confused when using these symbols. The symbols for less than (<)and greater than (>) can be referred to as arrows which always point to the smaller number. Another way to think of the symbols is to consider them sharks with open mouths that will only eat the largest number in an equation. Your students will even start drawing teeth inside the symbol!

Give students plenty of opportunities to use these symbols, through board work, partner work, and individual practice.

Place Value

Teach students place value and the correct way to read numbers. Explore what each number represents in terms of place value (see chart below). Start with numbers to 100, and then build from there. Students will recognize patterns in the numbers to help them learn all of the number names.

Example: For the number 381, the place values represent:

Hundreds	Tens	Ones	
3	8	1	300
			80
			1
			381

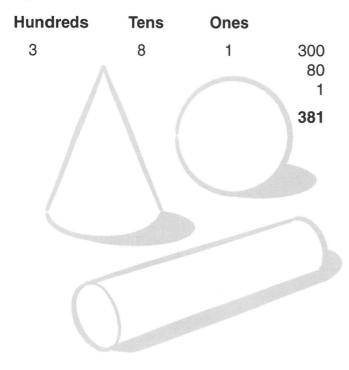

Before and After

Students need practice using mental math to figure out basic addition and subtraction equations such as add one (+1) or minus 1 (−1) for numbers greater than 18. For example, give a student the number 137 and tell him or her to add one. The student needs to know that number that follows 137 is 138. This does not seem like a difficult task to us, however when the number is presented out of context to a budding mathematician, it is an abstract concept requiring time to grasp. Try doing the calculations on the chalkboard, the overhead projector, or the number line and reinforce the experience by choral reading the problem. Once students are able to work with numbers in the ones place, introduce add 10 and minus 10. The next step would be to have the students calculate add 100 or minus 100. Students should be encouraged to use mental math procedures and calculate the answers in their heads.

Magnetic Money Tray

This is a great way to have the students practice their money counting skills. You will need a steel cookie sheet and some spare change (two quarters, three dimes, six nickels, and 15 pennies). Stick a small rectangle of magnetic tape on the back of each coin. Display the money from greatest to least value on the tray. Explain to students that they are going to make the date in change. Model this by showing how many ways this can be done. For example, if the date were October 16, how many ways could the date be shown? Combinations include a dime, a nickel and one penny; three nickels and a penny; or 16 pennies. Students take turns making the date in change. They love moving the magnetic money around on the tray.

Classroom Store

Setting up a classroom store gives students an incentive to do their work as well as practice their money skills. Use play money that looks like real currency. Assign money values to certain student jobs such as "complete and turn in science journal - 3¢" "read quietly for 15 minutes - 3¢" As a class you can decide whether certain classroom housekeeping chores such as alphabetizing library books by last names of the authors should be paid jobs. Assign values to those jobs. Have students keep their "money" in a special place—a pocket wall chart works well. Once a week, open the classroom store. Students count their money to figure out what they can afford to buy. The items in the store are priced in easy-to-add amounts so that students can exercise their mental math and estimation skills. Merchandise can be simple and inexpensive. You may wish to include some more "expensive" items like books to motivate students.

Coupons

Make an unusual and inexpensive learning tool for student practice of money skills. Cut coupons from local newspapers or mail advertisements and laminate them. Give students the coupons and a bag of change. Have them make change that matches the savings on the coupons.

Partner Penny Game

For more mental math exercise have students grab and count pennies. from a pouch containing 20 pennies. Students work with partners. One student takes a handful of pennies and counts aloud how many pennies he or she has in hand. The other student than figures out how many pennies remain in the bag. Remind students to check their answers by counting.

Dicey Numbers

Practice building numbers with dice. Ask students to roll the dice and then form the greatest numbers or smallest numbers possible. Start with two dice. For example, the student rolls a three and a six. The greatest number formed by the dice would be 63 and the lowest number would be 36. As students progress, add additional dice to the game.

Doubles Dice Game

Students take turns rolling two dice. When the students rolls doubles, they earn the total number they roll—either two, four, six, eight, or ten points. Students keep a running tally, and the first student who earns 50 points wins. The only catch is if they roll two sixes, they have to erase their entire score and start over.

Measurement

Foot ruler

Have students use their fingers, hands, and arms to measure objects around the room. Then have students draw around one of their feet (with or without shoes) onto a piece of paper to make a foot-ruler. Then they practice measuring objects around the room and the school to find out how many "feet" the objects measure. They will notice that different students get different measurements. Ask them why this might occur. Encourage students to recognize that not everyone has the same size foot, so that the the answers are not uniform. This can lead you into a discussion of the value of standard measuring tools.

Linking cubes

Using linking cubes, students find objects that are bigger and smaller than a unit you have defined. For example, the assignment could be to find something that is shorter than ten linking cubes in length, and something longer than 15 linking cubes in length. Make a class chart of all the items that the students found.

Teacher outline

Ask another teacher or your students to draw a life-sized outline of you onto a large piece of butcher paper. Teach estimation and measurement skills using the outline. Display it in front of the class. Divide students into groups of three or four. Ask students how many linking cubes tall they think you are. Have groups come up with an estimate. Record their estimates on a chart. Have one group at a time check its estimate, linking enough cubes to match their guess. As groups check their estimates, the remaining groups can change their estimate based on the information that has been learned. Students love this activity.

> We must go beyond what we were taught and teach how we wish we had been taught. We must bring to a life a vision of what a mathematics classroom should be . . . A richer mathematics program is also supported by an explosion of new mathematical knowledge—more mathematics has been created in this century than in all our previous history.
>
> —Miriam A. Leiva, <u>Curriculum and Evaluation Standards for School Mathematics, Addenda Series</u>

Place Value Games

Place-value blocks come in units of one, ten, hundreds, and thousands. They are useful manipulatives for students to use to explore place value, and they can be used to play educational games.

Have students build structures with the blocks, then total the "value" of the structures. Extend the activity by assigning a "value" to a building and seeing the different kinds of structures that the students build.

The object of the next game is to be the first player to collect a designated number above 100. Give a group of two to five students a pair of dice and a varied collection of place-value blocks in units of one, ten, and one hundred. Students take turns rolling the dice. The student who rolls the dice adds the digits on the top faces of the dice together, and collects that value of blocks. Each time he or she has ten 1-unit cubes, the cubes must be changed for a 10-unit stick. When a student collects ten, 10-unit sticks, they must be exchanged for a 100-unit block. When one of the students acquires the designated number, the game is over.

Word Problems

Go over many examples of word problems as a class and look at key words in word problems. Write some of these key math words on word strips and place them in a pile. Some key math words are *more than, less than, take away, how many more, how many are left,* and so on. Label a pocket chart with the headings *Addition word problems* and *Subtraction word problems*. Have each student choose a card with a math key word and place the card under the correct heading on the pocket chart. Then have students write their own word problems using the math key words. Team each student with a partner for a word-problem exchange.

Statistics and Probability

Talk to the students about probability in terms of what is most likely going to happen. Use the words *it is probably going to be . . .* Gather three or four chips of different colors with different quantities of each color, such as four red chips, seven white chips, ten blue chips, and one yellow chip. Have students count the chips to find out how many there are of each color and place them in a bag. Write the totals on the board. As chips are drawn from the bag, adjust the totals to reflect the quantities of each color that are still in the bag by subtracting. Students take turns picking chips. Students predict what color they think will emerge next. Record their predictions and record what was picked. Talk with the class about why certain chips are more likely or less likely to be picked.

Line of Symmetry

Symmetry is an important concept. Direct your students' attention to a large symmetrical object like the chalkboard. Draw a vertical line down the center and guide students to see that the shape of the blackboard on both sides of the line is the same size and shape. The vertical line is called the line of symmetry. There are many other objects that are the same on both sides of the line of symmetry as well. Have students find pictures of objects in a magazine that fit this description. Cut the pictures in half along the line of symmetry and glue one of the halves on a sheet of paper. Have students draw the missing half.

Symmetrical Cut-paper Designs

Students create their own symmetrical objects with paper. Fold a piece of colored construction paper in half lengthwise. The fold in the paper will form the line of symmetry of the design when the paper is opened. Students draw their designs on the folded paper and carefully cut out the designs. Open the cut-out and glue it to a sheet of contrasting colored paper.

Multiplication

Everyday objects can be used to teach the concepts of multiplication. Start teaching multiplication by looking at things that come in twos (eyes and ears); threes (tricycles and triangles); fours (passenger-car wheels); fives (fingers and toes); and sixes (six-packs of soda). Talk about how many are in each group and then relate that quantity to the whole. For example, one pair of eyes would represent two parts of one whole, because there are two eyes in the pair. One car would represent four parts of one whole because a passenger car has four wheels. Have students draw pictures to represent their findings. Compile the findings in a book of multiplication problems.

Division

Use food to teach division. Ask students how they would share one cookie between two people equally. Then ask how they would share the same cookie between three people or four people. Talk about the parts in relation to the whole. Have the students draw pictures of how they would divide the cookie.

Divide the class into groups of four. Give each group a cup of pretzels or small crackers. Ask students to divide the food evenly so that everyone in their groups gets a fair share.

Always have students draw pictures and/or write to show their reasoning. The exercise of explaining their reasoning helps them make sense of what they learn. Most modern math programs do not rely on drill and rote memorization facts—they rely on learning ways to think and solve problems.

Geometry Scavenger Hunt

Review shapes and their names with the class. Students go on a scavenger hunt to notice items in the room that match the shapes. Students draw pictures of what they find and label the shape(s). This can be done as a homework activity as well.

Shadow Theater

Give each student an 8-1/2" x 11" piece of paper. Have them fold the papers into four or eight squares, depending on how many questions you will ask. Tell students they are going to use their imaginations to guess what objects you are placing on the overhead projector. Place a cardboard screen around the overhead projector so that students cannot see the actual object you are projecting. Darken the room and place one object at a time on the projector screen. Students draw the objects they see or identify them in writing. Project geometric shapes as well as everyday items such as scissors, pencils, or paper clips.

Partner Pattern Game

This game requires knowledge of shape names. Students playing this game are also practicing giving and following verbal directions, and using describing words. Have students choose partners. Give each partner the same amount and variety of pattern blocks. (Different partner groupings can have different identical sets.) Place a divider between the partners. One partner makes a pattern then describes the shapes and locations of the components to the second partner. The person giving directions cannot look at the design of the person following the directions. The second partner tries to reproduce the design using only the verbal directions. When they have finished, they compare designs. You will all see some interesting results.

Calendar Skills

At the beginning of the month, put the class calendar together as a group so that the students participate and learn how the days relate to each other. Have students decorate the squares with the dates written on them or use commercial date cards. Then call the date numbers in order. Each student comes to the calendar and places his or her number in the correct location. This activity takes less than 15 minutes, but can be meaningful to the students. The calendar should be used daily for reference and practice. Other skills, such as location of the days of the week and general calendar skills should also be developed.

Name: _____ **Date:** _____

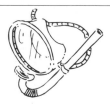

Exploring the Calendar

Directions: Create the calendar for one month. Use it to answer the questions below.

_____

Sunday	Monday	Tuesday	Wednesday	Thursday	Friday	Saturday

1. The 15th is on what day of the week? _____

2. The second Tuesday is the _____.

3. How many Fridays are there? _____

4. On what day of the week does this month start? _____

5. On what day of the week does this month end? _____

6. How many days are there in the month? _____

7. On what day will the first of next month be? _____

Make up your own three questions about the calendar. Ask a friend to answer them.

NUMBER CHART 1–100

1	2	3	4	5	6	7	8	9	10
11	12	13	14	15	16	17	18	19	20
21	22	23	24	25	26	27	28	29	30
31	32	33	34	35	36	37	38	39	40
41	42	43	44	45	46	47	48	49	50
51	52	53	54	55	56	57	58	59	60
61	62	63	64	65	66	67	68	69	70
71	72	73	74	75	76	77	78	79	80
81	82	83	84	85	86	87	88	89	90
91	92	93	94	95	96	97	98	99	100

PHYSICAL EDUCATION

Skills

Present activities to help students develop their skills as they are growing and changing. Mix partner and cooperative games to help the students learn to work together and have fun doing it. Physical education and other areas of the curriculum can be integrated to support the various learning styles of your students.

- **Locomotor**—walk backward; run in a tag game, run in a relay; hop 20 feet on dominant foot and 20 feet on non-dominant foot; hop to a simple musical rhythm; play hopscotch, beanbag hop, and similar games; jump evenly into the air from both feet; leap over a three-foot space; leap into the air while running; gallop 20 feet with the same foot leading; skip around cones on a five-foot line. Combination movements include pivoting around a foot and dodging in a dodge ball game.

- **Non-locomotor**—curl the body into a tight ball; swing and sway the body to a simple musical pattern; practice pushing and pulling while holding a partner's hands; attempt to twist the body in two directions at the same time; shake several parts of the body at the same time.

- **Manipulative movements**—strike two rhythm sticks together according to directions; throw a ball overhand and hit a target; throw a ball with one hand while the opposite foot is forward; kick a stationary ball; kick a moving ball; bounce a ball ten times; cross the horizontal bars without falling; serve to start a game of tetherball; catch a ball which has bounced off a wall; catch a fly ball in a beginning fistball game; return a ball to another square by hitting it with an open palm (two-square and four-square games); return a serve in a tetherball game; learn to bat a utility ball with one hand; play games of caroms, table golf, and maze.

- **Perceptual motor**—identify the right and left sides of one's body; differentiate between objects according to size, shape, and color; listen to and repeat a complex clapping rhythm.

- **Flexibility and agility**—crawl and walk over, under, and through obstacles on the floor; complete a challenge course involving bending; demonstrate a bend, a twist, a stoop, and a squat; demonstrate back flexibility by sitting on the floor, legs stretched in front, and reaching for the toes.

- **Muscular strength and endurance**—hang on a bar with a mixed grip; and, perform exercises to increase strength.

- **Cardiorespiratory endurance**—perform locomotor skills for increasing periods of time; jog for three minutes (some walking permitted); and, jump a rope held at various lengths.

- **Understanding and appreciating fitness**—understanding the basic principles of exercise; understand basic health principles related to exercise, cleanliness, and illness; and, understand what it means to be physically fit and how to maintain fitness.

- **Balance**—balance on tiptoes while moving around in big circles; walk forward on the balance beam; and, stand on a balance beam on one foot; extend arms like the wings of an airplane.

- **Body awareness**—move in a large group without touching; move fast and then slowly; change directions quickly, with stability; climb, grasp with the hands, and pull body around and through apparatus; participate in balancing activities while moving and while not moving.

- **Self-realization**—work toward the achievement of goals; explain what having a positive attitude toward learning new skills means; demonstrate the realization that several attempts or practice periods may be necessary to attain goals.

- **Self-expression**—role-play people, animals, and machines; understand accomplishment for self-satisfaction; create and demonstrate a rhythmic pattern.

- **Social behavior**—encourage play with at least two others; encourage and praise others frequently; begin to understand the meanings of constructive and non-constructive comments; learn to cooperate with teacher and classmates; take responsibility for own conduct; develop fellowship with others; accept constructive criticism as a cue for improvement; participate in rhythmics, team games, and sports.

Stretching

Start your physical education class with stretching. Always have students warm up first—it is an important health habit and will energize and motivate students. Once a routine is established, have students take turns leading the class.

Using Imagination

Students pretend they are trees or flowers, growing from a seed to a full flower in bloom. Have students hop like a frog, flutter like a butterfly, walk like a bear, or scuttle like a crab. Students love pretending they are animals.

I See game

Pick a relatively small enclosed area. You cue students with the phrase, "I see . . ." They answer, "What do you see?" You reply, "I see hopping." Immediately the students begin hopping. Other activities you could describe include jogging, skipping, and walking on tip-toes.

Four Square

You will need a four-square court where students can practice serving, hitting, and rotating. Introduce the game and explain the rules. Show students the court set-up. The player in square one is always the server and serves from behind the serve line. To serve the ball, drop and hit it underhanded after the first bounce. If the ball hits a line, the server is out. The player who receives the ball can direct it with an underhand hit to any square. Play continues until one player fails to return the ball or commits a fault.

Four Square Faults

- hitting the ball overhand or sidearm

- landing the ball on the line between the squares

- stepping into another square to play the ball

- catching or carrying a return volley

- allowing the ball to touch any part of the body except the hands

When a player misses or commits a fault, he or she moves to the end of the waiting line, and the players on the court move to fill empty squares, leaving the fourth square open. The person at the head of the line moves into square four to become a player.

> **We might cease thinking of school as a place, and learn to believe that it is basically relationships between children and adults, and between children and other children. The four walls and the principal's office would cease to loom so hugely as the essential ingredients.**
>
> **—George Dennison, <u>The Lives of Children</u>, 1969**

> **Nothing is more revealing than movement.**
>
> —Martha Graham, "The American Dance," in Virginia Steward, ed., <u>Modern Dance</u>, 1928

Parachute Play

A parachute is a piece of physical education apparatus that requires full-class participation and develops strength, coordination, and gross motor skills. Find a large area where you can play with the parachute. Open the parachute and have all your students hold its edge. Have everyone step back at the same time to extend and lift the parachute off the ground. Several activities for parachute play follow.

Parachute Bouncing

The class works together to bounce balls around the parachute by flapping the parachute. Different balls can be used, from tennis balls to beach balls, or more than one ball at a time. Extend the activity by playing music and bouncing the balls in time to the music.

Elevator

Start with the parachute at ground level. On the command "elevator up" students lift the chute overhead while keeping it stretched tight. On the command "elevator down," they lower the chute to the starting position. Reinforce body identification by announcing different elevator stops such as knees, waist, or shoulders.

Team ball

The object of this game is to get and keep a ball on the opponents' half of the parachute. Divide students into two equal teams on opposite sides of the parachute. Each team defends its territory by trying to keep the ball off its side of the parachute.

Making Popcorn

Explore gross motor movements by placing six to ten bean bags on the parachute. Shake the parachute to make the beanbags jump around like corn popping.

Cat and Mouse

This is a hide-and-seek game with a twist. One student is the mouse and another is the cat. The students who remain hold the parachute close to the ground and cheer the cat and mouse. The mouse goes under the parachute, and the cat on top of the parachute. The cat chases the mouse through the parachute. Make the game more challenging by blindfolding the cat or requiring the cat to close his or her eyes.

Catching

Teach students catching and throwing skills using different balls. Start with a handball (the kind of ball you use for dodge ball) or any other soft ball. Then use more difficult balls such as basketballs or footballs. The students work with partners to practice their catching and throwing skills. Increase throwing distances as students improve and develop their skills.

Kickball or Bootball

This game is played much like baseball. There are two teams with at least nine players on each team. Teams take turns kicking. A server rolls the ball to one kicker at a time. The kicker boots the ball and runs the bases. The team in the outfield tags a runner by hitting him or her with the ball or by throwing the ball to the base where the runner is heading. After three outs, teams switch places. The team with the most runs wins. Field positions are pitcher, catcher, first base, second base, shortstop, third base, right field, center field, and left field.

Freeze Tag

Tag develops students' running and dodging skills. Choose one to three students to be "it." The other students must run and dodge to avoid getting tagged by "it." Once they are tagged, they must "freeze." They cannot move until another student (not "it") tags and unfreezes them.

Hoop-a-Chain

This game develops balance and motor skills as well as reinforcing the need to work as a team. Explain that the students will form a circle and hold hands. One pair of students in the circle will join hands through a large hoop. The hoop will be passed around the circle without any students dropping hands, which means that students will have to move through the hoop to pass it around. When the hoop returns to its beginning point, the game is over.

You can make this a competitive game by dividing the class into groups of five to eight students who hold hands. You signal the start of each game with a whistle or clap. The students pass the hoops around the circles. The first team to move the hoop around the circle to reach its beginning point wins the game.

Vary this game by adding more hoops to the circle or by having groups of "chained" students move through stationary hoops.

Passing Line

Students form a line one behind the other. Instruct students to pass the ball to the people behind them. When the last person in line receives the ball, he or she goes to the front of the line and starts to pass the ball again. Variations of this game are using different-sized balls, and different kinds of ball passes such as overhead, between the legs, and to alternating sides.

Relays

Students are divided into four teams. If you don't have four equal teams, some students will need to run extra laps to make the race equal. Each student takes a turn participating in the relay race. Activities for a relay can include running, walking, jogging, hopping, skipping, or any other movement that is fun for the students. Each student runs, or walks, or jogs in turn. As the student crosses the line, he or she taps the next person to pass the turn. The team whose members complete the designated number of turns first wins the race. Relay races do not have to be competitive games. Your students will enjoy the teamwork and activity without needing a "winner."

You can add complexity to this activity by having students pass batons or carry beans balanced on a spoon, or requiring that students balance objects such as bean bags on top of their heads. These variations help students develop balance and coordination.

> **TIP!**
>
> *When your students are unfocused and antsy, take them to the playground or gym to run nonstop relays. Don't worry about who wins, just let the students run and run and run.*

SCIENCE AND HEALTH

Science

The goal of science education is that students develop observational skills and learn about life through science. The activities in which students participate should include classification, observing using the five senses, and designing and testing hypotheses. You act as a guide and allow students to explore and discover on their own.

Skills

- Explore, observe and organize objects.

- Use the five senses to analyze and describe.

- Propose a possible answer to a problem.

- Describe expected outcomes from information gathered from previous observations.

- Design simple investigations to test an hypothesis.

- Use skills for identifying problems, predicting, measuring, recording, summarizing, and describing.

- Make observations, gather and interpret data using appropriate tools.

- Compare relative weights and distances related to science activities.

- Select and manipulate science materials in a safe manner.

- Use spoken and written communications to communicate about data and procedures used in investigations.

- Recognize the differences between facts and hypotheses.

- Follow directions and safety procedures in all investigations.

- Use appropriate reading and language skills in comprehending science content.

KWL Chart

Many science, other curricular areas, and thematic units get a strong start with the use of a KWL chart. KWL stands for Know, Wonder, and Learned. It is an efficient way to introduce a unit. It gives you a good idea of what students already know about an idea, and therefore what information they still need, and what might pique their curiosity.

Take one large piece of butcher paper and divide it into three sections, labeling the separate sections Know, Wonder, or Learned, in that order from left to right, or use three sheets of easel paper, labeled individually Know, Wonder, or Learned.

First ask students what they know about a subject. Write down all the answers—even if what they "know" is incorrect.

Ask them what questions they have about the subject and write their questions in the Wonder section of the chart. You may find that filling in both the Know and Wonder sections simultaneously keeps the momentum of the discussion going well.

Leave the Learned section blank during the introduction phase of the unit. Keep the KWL chart(s) posted during the unit. Add to the Learned section as you finish different lessons, or as students make important discoveries.

Know	Wonder	Learned
rocks are hard we find them at the beach some are big and some are small	Why are rocks different colors? Why can we write with some rocks? Why are rocks sharp?	

Help students develop experiments that will allow them to discover the answers to their questions. When you have finished the topic, review the Learned section and add any important conclusions students reach.

Discovery Journal

Give students journals to take with them wherever they go, both inside and outside the classroom, with instructions to take notes of what they discover or observe during the day. You might assign a specific subject to observe. Students might note any questions that they may have. As these are personal journals, each one will be as unique as the student who writes it. During closing activities, students can share their discoveries. This activity fosters class discussions and provides you with another way to know what your students are curious about.

Phases of the Moon

For each student, you will need a yardstick, meter stick, or other long stick, a plastic foam ball, a craft stick, and masking tape. Each student will push the craft stick into the ball, then use masking tape to attach the other end of the craft stick to the end of a yardstick. The craft stick should be perpendicular to the yardstick. Darken the room. You hold a table lamp without the shade at your eye level to represent the sun. Students hold their sticks pointing toward the ceiling at 45° angles. The students pretend they're the Earth by standing in one spot and turning themselves around in circles in place for one complete rotation while observing the effect of the light on the plastic foam ball attached to the sticks in their hands. They will see how the sun and earth relate to create the phases of the moon.

Weather

Start the year with a thematic unit that includes weather. An introduction to the four seasons beginning with fall is perfect for September (or beginning with summer if your school year starts in July). You could revisit this theme throughout the year as the seasons change. Weather is a fascinating topic with many ideas that can be covered. Here are few ideas you can include in a weather section.

- There are many kinds of weather.

- Moving air is called wind.

- Rain is water in the air that falls to earth in drops.

- Snow is frozen water that falls to earth in flakes.

- The sun warms the earth.

- Weather affects how we live.

- We can see changes in the weather.

Make Your Own Cloud

Put three inches of hot water in a bottle. Put an ice cube on the top of the bottle. As the hot water evaporates, the ice cools it and a cloud is formed.

Make Your Own Thermometer

Have students track the temperature throughout the day and discuss what will cause the changes. (Find a worksheet for this activity on page 53.)

Make a Rainbow

You need a garden hose, water, and sunshine. Stand with your back to the sun and spray the water in a fine mist away from the sun. Have your students look in the mist for a rainbow.

45

What's in the Bag?

Using the five senses, students make predictions about what is in a mystery bag. Fill plastic zipper bags with edible items such as apples, oranges, cookies, chips, or peanuts. Put the plastic zipper bag inside a small brown paper bag to hide its contents. Divide students into groups of three or four. Give each group a bag. Tell them not to touch or pick up the bags. Based on their senses of smell, students make and record their predictions of what is in the bags. Next, shake each bag so that students can hear the contents and can either confirm or change their predictions. Allow students to reach inside the bags to use their senses of touch. Confirm or change predictions. Next, one person from each group volunteers to taste the mystery item and makes a prediction based on taste. Finally students use their senses of sight to verify their predictions. Make sure that none of your students have known allergies to the foods you are having them taste.

Sense of Smell

Explain how our senses help us make observations and learn about our world. Collect six empty film canisters with tops. Punch a hole in each top with a nail. Number the canisters. Put a different aromatic object in each canister such as crushed garlic, cotton balls soaked in vanilla, lime-scented cologne, rose-scented perfume, or loose cloves. Put the lids on the canisters. Students use their senses of smell to identify the odor of the sample. and record their guesses on a data sheet. Reveal what the samples were. Tally how many students correctly identified each smell.

Plants from Seeds

Talk about what living things need (sunlight, water, and air) and how they are different from non-living things. Grow plants in the classroom from seeds, planting them in dirt in plastic foam cups. Students label their cups with their names, the dates, and the kinds of plants, and monitor the growth of their plants, watering them as needed. Every other day students measure and chart the growth of their plants.

Seeds Have Potential

This activity is a simple approach to the complex concept of biotic potential. It is a good follow up to the *Plants from Seeds* activity above. You will need:

- brown paper or brown paper bags

- plastic knives (one knife for each group of three to four students)

- apples (one apple for each group of three to four students)

- a data sheet

Talk about where seeds come from, why they are important, and what a seed looks like. Combine and compare student answers as a class and come to a general understanding of the concept of seeds. Give one apple to each group of three or four students. Ask students to locate the seeds in the apple and record how many they find on a data sheet. Students then predict the number of plants that could grow from each seed. Remind students of their experiences growing plants in plastic foam cups—one seed could grow one plant. Encourage students to talk about their observations and ask questions, such as *Why are apple seeds important?* and *How many apple trees do you think might grow if all the seeds were planted?* Eat the apples when you have concluded the activity. Further this investigation with study and discussion of other fruit such as peaches, oranges, tomatoes, or vegetables, such as peppers and cucumbers.

Animal Classification

Collect a large number of plastic animals. Talk about classification as a way scientists organize information about things they find in nature. Show students the plastic animals. Tell students that they will classify the animals by how they move—on the land, in the air, or in the water. Ask students what they observe.

Put three large hoops on the floor, slightly overlapping them, to create a large Venn diagram. Label the areas of the Venn diagram: land; air; water; land and air; land and water; air and water; land, air, and water. Have students take turns placing animals in the correct section of the diagram. Animals that fit more than one category are placed in the overlapping sections of the hoops to represent that they belong to both groups.

Fingerprints

Each person is a one of a kind. Prove this to your students by showing them that their fingerprints are unique. Have them draw two rows 1" x 1" squares on a piece of paper and label the squares, one row for the left hand fingers—left little, left ring, left middle, left index, left thumb, and one row for the right hand fingers—right thumb, right index, right middle, right ring, right little. Tell students to take their fingerprints by the following method.

- Rub a pencil tip on a piece of paper until it makes a large black mark.

- Rub the pad of your index finger on the black mark.

- Stick a one-inch piece of clear tape to your index finger.

- Remove the tape. Place it on the record page.

- Look at the pattern.

- Do the same thing for every finger on each hand.

Left Hand	little finger	ring finger	middle finger	index finger	thumb	
	thumb	index finger	middle finger	ring finger	little finger	**Right Hand**

What's the Matter?

Hold up a piece of chalk and ask the students to describe the properties. Be sure they include color, size, shape, texture, weight, hardness, and odor. Discuss the physical properties of other objects in the room. Tell students they will make a mystery substance called *oobleck* by Dr. Seuss and they will have to decide how to describe it.

Cover work surfaces. Provide each work station with pencil and paper to write questions and record observations, in addition to supplies that students can use to make *oobleck* and tools to further their investigations such as potato mashers, eggbeaters, plastic spoons, straws, and toothpicks. The *oobleck* recipe follows.

- four boxes of cornstarch (approximately 58 ounces)

- six cups of water (approximately 1-1/2 cups of water per box of cornstarch)

- green food coloring

Add food coloring to one quart of water (four cups). Pour the green water into a mixing bowl and add the cornstarch and another two cups of water. Swirl and tip the bowl to level the contents. Set the bowl aside for a few minutes. Slip your fingers under and lift from the bottom of the bowl to the top to mix the oobleck. Keep mixing until the oobleck is of an even consistency. The oobleck should feel like a solid but flow when you tip the bowl. It dries quickly and brushes off easily. Ask students to describe the properties of *oobleck*.

Natural Disasters

Talk with students about the kinds of natural disasters that can occur in your area. Discuss the school's disaster plan, what the students will be expected to do in an emergency, and what they can expect from you. Frequently practice any safety drills so that they become second nature to your students and you.

> **TIP!**
>
> Introduce the "What's the Matter" lesson by reading the story *Bartholomew and the Oobleck* by Dr. Seuss (Random House, 1949).

Changes

Plan for this activity to take place over three to five weeks. Tell students that they are going to be observing and discussing changes. Students need to bring in two closed jars from home. In one jar they will place something that they think will change, and in the other jar, something that they think will not change. Label the jars accordingly and place them in an area where the students will have easy access to observe them. Have students begin daily journals. As the weeks progress, students will be excited about the changes that are occurring in front of them. Discuss the changes that are occurring and why. Talk about the items that are not changing as well.

Design a Science Experiment

Model how to do a science experiment. Decide as a class what idea you would like to test such as "What happens to air as it is heated?" Plan and carry out the class science experiment.

Here is one way to test the question. Take a lightweight plastic bag and a hair dryer. Hold the open bag upside-down over hair dryer. Turn hair dryer on at a hot setting. After a few seconds, turn off the hair dryer and let go of the bag.

Give students an opportunity to plan their own science experiments. Following these steps will enable your students to be successful.

- Think of a hypothesis (an idea to test).

- Put it in the form of a question you can test.

- Plan your experiment.

- List the materials you will need.

- List the steps you will follow.

- Do the experiment

- Record data.

- Come to a conclusion. The conclusion should answer the question being tested.

Health

Skills

- Practice good grooming, desirable personal health habits, and good posture.

- Be physically active.

- Take care of teeth. Choose snacks that promote dental health.

- Make healthful food choices according to food groups. Discuss reasons that food choices were made.

- Identify the occupations of people who grow and prepare food.

- Recognize safe and unsafe food handling and preparation.

- Explore personal feelings related to likes and dislikes.

- Compare and contrast ways to express emotions responsibly and irresponsibly.

- Identify common medications and their uses.

- Differentiate between substances that may be helpful and those which are harmful.

- Tell about making choices and their health and safety.

- Know to report to a responsible adult any offer of an unknown substance or known harmful substance.

- Describe how germs enter the body.

- Identify practices that cause, spread, or control disease.

- Identify sources for assistance with a health problem.

- Discuss services provided by different health professionals.

- Identify conditions in the environment that may affect health.

- Differentiate between good and bad touching.

- Identify and practice good safety procedures when traveling to and from school.

- Demonstrate appropriate behavior during emergency drills.

- Observe safety rules for the playground.

- Discuss emergency-preparedness for both school and home.

> **The world looks so different after learning science.**
>
> **For example, trees are made of air, primarily. When they are burned, they go back to air, and in the flaming heat is released the flaming heat of the sun which was bound in to convert the air into tree. [A]nd in the ash is the small remnant of the part which did not come from air, that came from the solid earth, instead.**
>
> **These are beautiful things, and the content of science is wonderfully full of them. They are very inspiring, and they can be used to inspire others.**
>
> **—Richard Feynman**

49

Food Pyramid

Present the food pyramid. Talk about the different food groups and the recommended daily servings for each. Discuss which foods belong in each group. Use pictures of food and a large pyramid display to present the concept. Have students make their own food pyramids. Cut pyramid shapes from construction paper. Model the pyramid divisions on the blackboard so that the students can add them to their pyramids. Have students look through magazines for examples of food from the different food groups to glue on their pyramids. Punch holes in the top of the pyramids and suspend them from the ceiling using fishing line to create a bright display.

Making Healthy Choices

Have students plan a healthy breakfast, lunch, dinner, or snack. Remind them of what choices are healthy ones, to use foods from different food groups, and that fats and sweets should be eaten sparingly. Students draw their choices on a paper plate or write about them telling why they chose each item.

Make Fruit Salad

Teach your students how to make healthy snacks. Talk about the different vitamins and minerals our bodies need to stay healthy. Ask them to bring in different kinds of fruit they take turns to wash, slice, and cut into a large bowl. Orange juice can be added to give it more flavor and to keep some of the fruit from turning brown. Serve the fruit salad to the class.

Apple Smiles

Cut apples into quarters and cut the cores out. Students spread peanut butter on one side of their apple quarters. They look at their smiles in a mirror, and using mini-marshmallows to represent their teeth, replicate their mouths. When students have finished, they can compare their apple smiles with those of their classmates and then eat their smiles!

Use and Misuse of Substances

Talk to students about smoking, alcohol, and drugs. Talk about what each of these does to the human body. Discuss the benefits of prescribed medicine when used correctly. Discuss what students should do if someone offers them any of these substances, or any substances with which they are not familiar.

Write situations on cards posing dilemmas students could face. Have students choose a partner. Students draw cards and role play the situation on the card. A card could provide a situation like this sample. "An older girl at school offers you a cigarette. What do you do?"

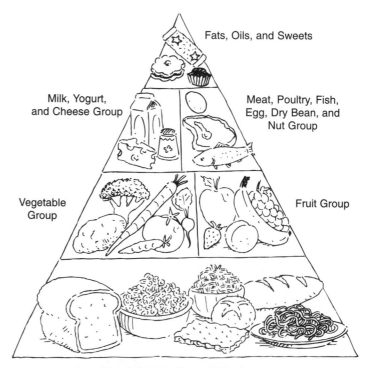

Fats, Oils, and Sweets

Milk, Yogurt, and Cheese Group

Meat, Poultry, Fish, Egg, Dry Bean, and Nut Group

Vegetable Group

Fruit Group

Bread, Cereal, Rice, and Pasta Group

> **Be true to your teeth, then they'll never be false to you.**
>
> —Soupy Sales

Recycling

Teach students the importance of recycling. Discuss that there are not enough places to store our trash and why recycling is necessary. Brainstorm a list of items that can be recycled. Start recycling in your own classroom. Place cardboard boxes around the room with labels for paper, can, and bottle recycling. Talk to the students about where the items are taken and how they are recycled.

Clean Up Litter

Take a walking field trip to a local park. Sit in a circle with your class and discuss the surroundings. Talk about litter, what it does to our environment, and what students can do about it. If the park is messy, have students pick up trash, and throw it away and/or collect recyclables. The students are doing their parts to care for the environment. After the students have finished, sit in a circle and talk about their experiences. Brainstorm ways that the students could make the community more aware of the importance of a clean environment. Possible ideas could be holding a can drive, making posters for local businesses, of having a regular clean-up-the-park-day.

Safety, Accident Prevention, and Emergency Services

Discuss the importance of being safe and how we can prevent accidents from happening. Give students certain situations to role play. Talk about what to do in an emergency. Make sure the students understand that 911 is only to be called in an emergency. When they need help, there are trained professionals to help them. Talk about the local police station, fire department, hospitals, and other emergency and community services in your area. Arrange field trips for students to learn more about jobs in the community.

51

Name: _____ **Date:** _____

_____
Topic

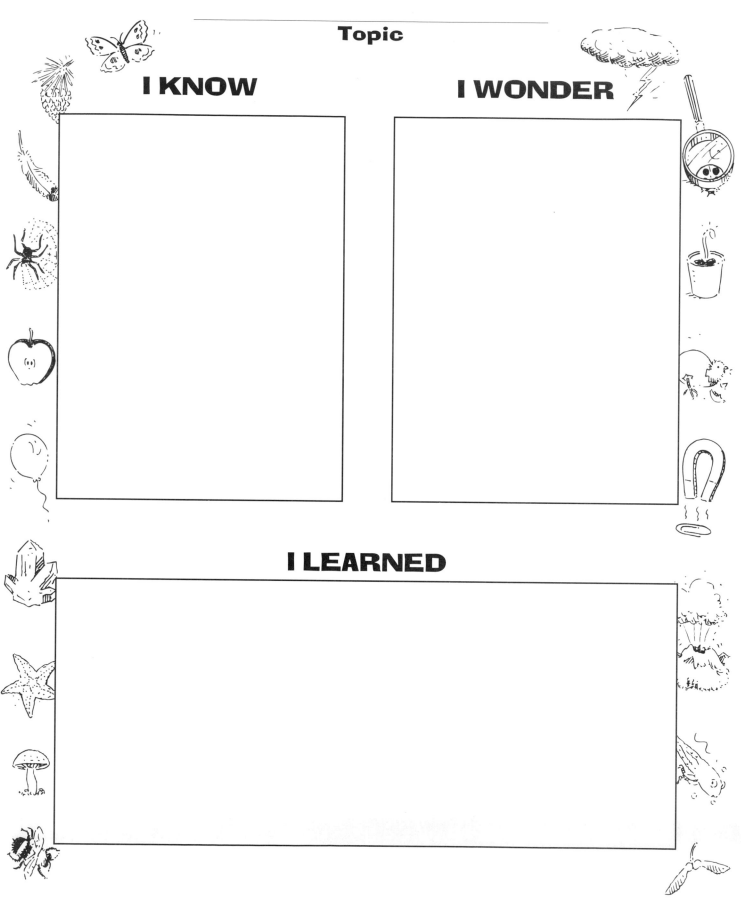

I KNOW

I WONDER

I LEARNED

FS122004 Getting Ready to Teach Second Grade

MAKE YOUR OWN THERMOMETER

Cut out the thermometer shape at the left along the thick outer line. Glue it to construction paper. Cut out the slits marked with a dotted line. Write your name on the back.

Color the strip to the right red below the line. Leave the part above the line white.

Cut along the dashed line.

Tuck the ends of the strip into the slits on the thermometer. The red part of the strip should be tucked into the slit marked with a star. Move the strip up and down.

The top of the red line marks the temperature.

53
reproducible

SOCIAL STUDIES

Skills

- Locate information in a variety of media including printed matter, electronic media, graphic materials, personal observation, and other people.

- Interpret information presented graphically.

- Arrange or present information to improve communication and learning.

- Identify various natural and human-made features illustrated on maps and/or globes such as land, bodies of water, streets, and bridges.

- Identify, describe, and use cardinal directions, and the mapmaking conventions such as equator, title, legend, and compass rose.

- Construct maps for specific purposes. Identify, describe, and read maps.

- Compare and contrast ideas about the same issue from different sources.

- Apply information to new situations.

- Identify or state problems and propose solutions.

- Develop personal and group values based on individual responsibility and ethical conduct.

- In the United States, learn the meaning of the Pledge of Allegiance; learn to sing *The Star-Spangled Banner*.

- Cooperate with others in planning individual and group work.

- Adjust individual behavior to the needs, problems, and hopes of others in order to work together effectively.

Social Studies Activities

Family History

Students make a family tree about their families. Their grandparents are the roots, their parents the trunks, and they and their siblings the branches, each sibling represented by a branch. This assignment lends itself well to homework, because parents or caretakers would be able to help complete the assignment.

Grandparent Interviews

Brainstorm with the class about what they would like to know about life in other times. Make a list of questions that students could ask their grandparents, elderly neighbors, or friends of the family. Photocopy the list of questions as an interview sheet for your students. Students could ask when and where the older people were born, what toys they played with or hobbies they had when they were younger, and what they liked and did not like about school. Have students record this information on the interview sheet. Students can share what they learned about their grandparents or life in a different era. A class graph of any statistical information the students gathered could be made. It might show the years that the grandparents were born, recreational activities, or favorite school subjects.

Personal Time Lines

Students make personal time lines starting with the year they were born through the present. For each year the student will include at least one event that happened in the world or in his or her personal life. Students combine words and pictures to add the events to their time lines.

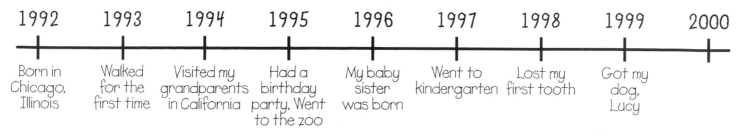

1992	1993	1994	1995	1996	1997	1998	1999	2000
Born in Chicago, Illinois	Walked for the first time	Visited my grandparents in California	Had a birthday party. Went to the zoo	My baby sister was born	Went to kindergarten	Lost my first tooth	Got my dog, Lucy	

Students need more than facts. They need to understand the relationships between "facts" and whose interests certain "facts" serve. They need to question the validity of the "facts," to ask questions such as "why" and "how." They need to know how to find information, to solve problems, to express themselves in oral and written language so their opinions can be shared with, and have an influence on, broader society. It is only through such an approach that students can construct their own beliefs, their own knowledge.

—Bob Peterson "What Should Children Learn?: A Teacher Looks at E.D. Hirsch" in <u>Rethinking Schools An Agenda for Change</u>

Geography Center

Set up a geography center which contains maps, globes, atlases, compasses, and information about different areas of the world. After students have had some exploration time at the center, present a mini-lesson about map conventions, such as recognizing bridges, land, bodies of water, and using a legend.

Make Maps of the School

Tell students that maps are the bird's-eye view of a place. Discuss components of maps and tell students they will be making individual maps of the school. Students must decide what they are going to include on their maps. Refresh student memories with a tour of the school while they take notes of places. Then students pretend that they are going to take someone around the school and make a map for the visitor. Extend the activity by taking a first-grade class on a tour, using the maps.

Flag

Study the national flag and teach students what the colors and shapes represent. The study of flag history and symbolism is called vexillology. Provide cloth scraps, and other art materials for students to use to make their own flags using colors that have meaning to them arranged in a personal design. Students write a paragraph to explain what their flags represent.

Good Citizen Book

Discuss with the class what a good citizen does. Some ideas are treating all people equally, following the laws, voting, and being active in the community. Make a *Good Citizen Book* by writing the class ideas, adding illustrations, and binding the papers together.

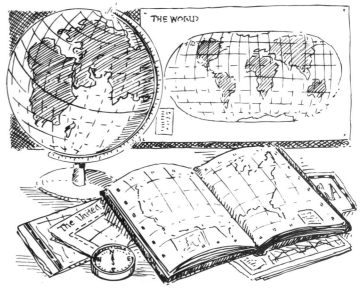

Ethnic Food

Incorporate cooking into classroom activities. Students talk about their favorite foods. Make a chart and graph student favorites. Ask students to talk to their parents about food that is important to the culture of their families. Students bring recipes from home to compile into a class book. Pick a day for an international potluck meal and invite parents to bring family food specialties, and to talk about their special dishes. Bring a special dish from your family's culture to share with the class.

TIP!

Give your students sufficient time to think of the answer to a question you ask. Most second-grade students do not think as fast as adults, and need several seconds to process a question in order to respond correctly.

Questioning

One of the great gifts you can give your students is the gift of questioning. It is essential to the development of thinking.

How you question can lead your students to develop higher level thinking abilities. Use questions that require more than a yes or no answer. Use questions to check comprehension, encourage students to support their opinions, to provide opportunities for them to apply knowledge.

We the peoples of the United Nations, determined to save succeeding generations from the scourge of war, which twice in our lifetime has brought untold sorrow to mankind, and to reaffirm faith in fundamental human rights, in the dignity and worth of the human person, in the equal parts of men an women and of nations large and small . . . and for these ends to practice tolerance and live together in peace with one another as good neighbors . . . have resolved to combine our efforts to accomplish these aims.

—Preamble to the Charter of the United Nations

Sample questions you can use to encourage your students to develop their thinking follow.

How did you find that answer?

How do you think the ice will change? Why?

How was the wolf able to destroy the pig's house of sticks blew down? . . . Why do you think it fell apart so easily?

Twenty Questions

Encourage students to formulate clear questions. The age-old game of Twenty Questions is a great way to begin teaching how to use questions to narrow possible answers. Model good questioning techniques.

Student: I am thinking of a number.

You: Is it under 100?
Student: Yes.

You: Is it under 50?
Student: No.

You: Is it between 51 and 75?
Student: Yes.

You: Is it between 51 and 60?
Student: Yes

You: Is it odd?
Student: Yes.

You: Is it above 55?
Student: No.

You: Is it 55?
Student: Yes!!

TECHNOLOGY

Technology requirements are changing daily. A general overview of the skills in this area is listed here for reference.

Skills

Industrial technology - construction projects
- Learn to interpret plans for constructing a project.

- Learn dimensional sequence: thickness, width, length.

- Use tools safely and properly.

- Develop an awareness of assembly techniques, and the relationship between raw materials and finished products.

Computer technology
- Handle the hardware in appropriate ways.

- Develop familiarity with the computer keyboard.

- Use basic software tools and processes appropriately.

- Become familiar with drawing and processing software.

Technology Activities

Invention Center

Have an Invention Center where students create new inventions with the pieces that have been taken apart at the Take-apart Center. Students can write about what they made and what it might be used for.

> "Why," said the Dodo, "the best way to explain it is to do it."
>
> —Lewis Carroll, <u>Alice in Wonderland</u>, Chapter 11

Take-apart Center

Give students an opportunity to explore how things are put together by supplying materials they can take apart like old clocks, old phones, and old appliances. Find the items to take apart at garage sales, second-hand stores, or request donations from friends and the parents of your students.

Set up your center with tools students will need, such as screwdrivers and pliers. Provide small boxes such as shoe boxes where students can store their projects between work sessions. Supply any tools that students might need. Students can take apart any item of their choice, examining and exploring the pieces. When they are finished, put the pieces into a plastic zipper bag. The students write a full description of what they looked at, and the things they discovered.

Keyboarding Skills

Teach students how to use the keyboard of the computer correctly—pushing on the letters, not banging them. Let them familiarize themselves with the locations of the letters. You could also identify the home keys—the left-hand keys are *a s d f* and the right hand keys *j k l ;*. Your school may have a software program for teaching typing that your students would enjoy.

VISUAL AND PERFORMING ARTS

Visual Arts

Skills

- Name, recognize, and describe colors, lines, shapes, values, and textures in art and objects in the environment.

- Observe the design principles of repetition, rhythm, and balance in art and in the environment.

- Observe that things look different under varying conditions.

- Express ideas and feelings about works of art and objects in nature.

- In the creation of personal artwork, demonstrate personal expressions, original concepts, and expressive qualities and moods.

- Use varied subject matter such as people, animals, plans, places, and events.

- Express the following on two-dimensional surfaces: overlapping of forms; variations in color, size, shape, and texture; and, repetition of line, shape, and color.

- Use a variety of drawing techniques: continuous line or action drawing; decorative, imaginative, or realistic styles; and, varied effects with the points and sides of crayons, pencils, and chalk.

- Use a variety of painting techniques: dry and wet brush; stippling; spatter painting; finger painting; color mixing; and, crayon-resist washes.

- Model and construct three-dimensional forms with a sense of relative proportion and emphasis using clay, bread dough, and other materials.

- Apply basic principles of relief printing, including additive (building up a design) and subtractive (carving out a design) methods.

- Use contrasting colors in personal artwork: light and dark; bright and dull; and, warm and cool.

- Consider and use all the art space available in the format provided.

- Organize objects of varying shapes, sizes, and textures into a three-dimensional arrangement.

- Grow in the ability to work with craft processes such as weaving, stitchery, and paper mâché.

- Create artwork based on images from the visual environment, memory, and from the imagination.

- Take good care of supplies.

> **Art teaches nothing, except the significance of life.**
>
> —Henry Miller, "Reflections on Writing," The Wisdom of the Heart, 1941

58

Visual Art Activities

This drawing cannot be completed quickly, and the finished pictures may not closely resemble hands. That is okay, because the students are learning how to look. Next students draw their shoes. Have students put their shoes on the table and again, looking at the contours, draw the shoes, without looking at their papers, nor lifting pencil from paper. Any object can be drawn this way.

Color Wheel

The primary colors are red, yellow, and blue. With white, they form all other colors. Put the following information on the board—red + yellow = orange, yellow + blue = green, and blue + red = purple.

Provide hands-on practice mixing colors and making color wheels using the worksheet on page 65. Begin by having the students paint the areas numbered 1, 3, and 5 red, yellow, and blue using tempera paint or watercolors. Then explain that the colors in sections 2, 4, and 6, are the secondary colors, mix them and paint them in the correct sections. Provide many painting exploration opportunities using different media such as water colors, tempera paints, and chalk mixed with water.

Craft Sticks

Students can create beautiful wood projects using craft sticks and white or wood glue. Show students the materials they will be using, and give a quick demonstration of how to apply a moderate amount of glue. Brainstorm ideas of what students could make. Some suggestions are picture frames, model airplanes, houses, or animals. Supply craft sticks, glue, and paint and let the students construct original projects.

Collages

Give students magazines and ask them to cut out pictures according to a specific theme. Possible themes are *myself, family, friends, winter,* or the theme you are studying. Students pick their own pictures and decide how to arrange them. Encourage students to overlap pictures, to put pictures next to each other that make interesting contrasts, and to fill as much of the paper as possible. Have them experiment how they will arrange the pictures before they glue any to the paper.

Sponge Paintings

Explore overlapping of forms and repetition of shape by painting with sponge shapes. Use meat trays or other small flat trays as paint holders. Prepare them with a damp paper towel folded to fit the tray (the institutional brown paper towel will serve very well). Squeeze a small amount of liquid tempera onto the damp paper towel and spread it around to make a thin layer of paint. Students use the trays like stamp pads, placing damp sponges lightly into the paint to coat them, and then stamping the shape onto paper.

Contour Drawing

To introduce the concept of line and form use contour drawing. Contour drawing is line drawing—putting on paper only the lines that can be seen. The students can start by drawing their hands. They rest the hands they do not write with next to their paper. With the other hand they begin to draw what the lines and curves of their hands, never lifting the pencil off the paper and not looking at the paper—only at their hands.

Paper Plate Mask

Students decorate the backs of paper plates to create masks based on books they are reading such as *Where the Wild Things Are* by Maurice Sendak (Harper Collins, 1992) or *The Mixed-Up Chameleon* by Eric Carle (Harper Collins, 1984). Students cut holes in the plates to see through. Punch two holes at the outer edge of the plate (at 3:00 and at 9:00 if the plate were a clock). Thread ribbon or yarn for the students to tie the mask on.

Weaving

Cut a 7" by 10" rectangle out of cardboard for each student. Cut half-inch slits every half inch along the top and the bottom of the cardboard to create a loom. Prepare the looms by stringing lengths of yarn vertically from top to bottom by sliding the yarn into the slits. Then students take another piece of yarn and weave it over and under the vertical lengths of yarn. In the opposite direction the pattern will be under and over the vertical lengths of yarn. Do not pull the yarn too tight. To change yarn color tie another color of yarn to the length they are working with, making a simple square knot.

When the board is covered completely with yarn, the student has finished. Tie off the ends and remove the weaving from the board. Cut the loops and the student has a finished woven rug.

Sculptures from Reusables

Collect reusable packaging materials wherever you can find them. A collection of materials such as bubble wrap, plastic foam trays, milk and egg cartons, plastic lids, yogurt containers, cardboard tubes, and boxes can be used to make large sculptures. Provide glue, brads, and staplers to attach pieces together Have students paint them when they are finished. Your students can also use the sculpture they make as a base to finish with papier mâché.

Art History Activities

Art museums in metropolitan areas frequently offer resources and programs for teachers including couses in art techniques, educational tours of the museum, and a lending program of photos or slides for classroom use.

There are many books about teaching art history to children and ways to improve art teaching in the classroom. Many are organized around themes that may fit in well with your instructional program.

Your local library will have books with reproductions of drawings and paintings created by the masters. Show them to your students and discuss the composition of the works and what is special about them. Ask students to talk and write about what they see. Have them choose favorite pictures and make copies of them in paint, crayon, colored pencil, or marker.

Some useful art reference materials:

Come Look With Me Series by Gladys S. Blizzard (Thomasson-Grant Inc.)

Enjoying Art With Children (1990)

Exploring Landscape Art with Children (1992)

Animals in Art (1992)

The World of Art through the eyes of artists Series by Wendy and Jack Richardson (Children's Press)

Animals (1991)

Cities (1991)

Entertainers (1991)

Families (1991)

The Natural World (1991)

Water (1991)

Portraits of Women Artists for Children Series by Robyn Montana Turner (Little, Brown and Company, 1992)

Seasonal

Many holidays that are celebrated during the year lend themselves to art lessons. Listed below are a few ideas for different holidays. Incorporate crafts from different cultures in creating a multicultural curriculum. Use some of these craft ideas as a basis for an art lesson focusing on a skill that is in your curriculum.

> We have to regard it as our sacred responsibility to unfold and develop each individual's creative ability as dim as the spark may be and kindle it to whatever flame it may conceivably develop.
>
> —V. Lowenfeld, <u>Basic Aspects of Creative Thinking</u>, 1961

September
Grandparent's Day - picture frames, self portraits

October
Columbus Day - craft stick ships

Halloween - ghost, haunted house

November
Veteran's Day - paper, awards of honor

Thanksgiving - still life drawing of a cornucopia

December
Kwanzaa - harvest picture

Hanukkah - make dreidels

Christmas - pop-up cards

January
New Years Day - confetti, party hats

Martin Luther King, Jr./Black History Month - *I Have a Dream* mobiles

February
Chinese New Year - paper lanterns

Valentine's Day - heart baskets

Presidents' Day - silhouettes

March
St. Patrick's Day - paper stained-glass window designs

April
Easter - dye eggs

Spring - floral paper mosaic

May
May Day - maypole

Mother's Day - origami flowers

Cinco de Mayo - flags of Mexico

June
Father's Day - paper tie

Flag Day - class or group flags

July
Fourth of July - star-spangled banner

August
Summer - sand painting

Anytime projects
- Cut-paper collage
- Sponge painting
- Yarn painting
- Paper-bag puppets

Music

- Differentiate between the pulse and the rhythm of a melody.

- Recognize singing in tune.

- Identify accented and unaccented beats or pulses.

- Identify identical, similar, and contrasting phrases.

- Recognize repetition of identical musical phrases and contrast of different musical phrases.

- Recognize songs in major and minor keys.

- Recognize differences in vocal tone quality.

- Identify certain orchestral instruments by sound.

- Sing with improving tone quality and accuracy of pitch and rhythm.

- Match pitches on a descending minor third.

- Sing patterns of rhythm accurately.

- Sing a complete musical phrase in one breath.

- Sing while accompanied by a countermelody that is played or sung.

- Select an appropriate tempo for a familiar song.

- Play songs by memory.

- Play a musical instrument to the beat of the music to accompany songs.

- Identify chord changes.

- Select appropriate percussion instruments to accompany a song.

- Use arm movements to show the contour of a melody.

- Use body movements to differentiate between the pulse and the rhythm of a melody.

- Respond to music with two-impulse locomotor movements such as galloping and skipping.

- Create movements to demonstrate identical or contrasting phases.

- Express emotion through movement.

- Identify patterns of melody and rhythm written in staff notation.

- Recognize longer patterns of rhythm written in blank notation.

- Identify identical phrases from notation.

- Improvise melodies on tonal instruments and rhythms on percussion instruments.

- Create symbols for identical phrases.

- Create movements to dramatize mood.

- Relate specific selections of music to areas identified on the map and globe.

- Learn about specific composers and their music.

- Demonstrate appropriate audience behavior at live performances.

Expose students to different varieties of music, from classical to contemporary and accustom them to listen intently to music. Instruct them in musical elements that will increase their appreciation and understanding of the different styles and forms.

Experience Music

Talk about the different styles and moods of music. Choose a composer and play different pieces of his or her work that reflect different tones and moods. Have students draw as they are listening. If you have students begin new pictures with each different musical piece, their drawings may reflect the different music. Put together a book for each student of art work done while listening to a particular composer.

Learn Instrument Names

Introduce the different instruments played in a piece of music. Talk about the instrument families—woodwinds, brass, and percussion. Listen to music that highlights a particular instrument or instruments. An enjoyable piece of symphonic music is *Peter and the Wolf* which uses orchestral instruments to create characters and tell a story. Invite community musicians to perform for your students, or take your students on a field trip to hear a symphony matinee.

Musical Cues

Use music to signal starting and stopping activities. Turn on the music when students begin their assignments. When the music stops, students know that they must stop what they are doing to get ready for the next activity.

Music to Teach Concepts

Use music to teach concepts such as capitalization, punctuation, and reinforce reading skills. Choose some of your class' favorite songs and write the words to the music on charts so the class can practice reading the words as they sing.

Chants Teach Rhythm

Simple jump rope chants teach students a sense of rhythm. Chant them as students jump rope or do other activities. Have students make up their own words to the chants using the same rhythm. Here are two simple jump rope chants:

Teddy Bear, Teddy Bear
turn around.
Teddy Bear, Teddy Bear
touch the ground.
Teddy Bear, Teddy Bear
tie your shoe.
Teddy Bear, Teddy Bear
that will do.

Kindergarten, first grade,
second grade, third grade,
fourth grade, fifth grade,
sixth grade, seventh grade,
eighth grade, ninth grade,
tenth grade, eleventh grade,
twelfth grade,
she's graduated!

Definitions of musical terms

Rhythm - The beats and organization of the music

Melody - The main line of a piece of music

Form - The structure of the piece of music

Harmony - The added lines in a piece of music

Dynamics - How loudly or softly the piece is played

Mood - The emotional feel of a piece

Clapping

Clapping is an easy way to practice rhythm and patterns with your students. Have the students follow your claps ("my turn, your turn"). Start slowly, clapping a four- to six-beat rhythm. As students are comfortable and confident, clap your beats faster. Talk with the students about how the rhythm changes when you change the speed of your clapping. Allow your students to lead the clapping patterns also.

Humming Patterns

Practice humming with students by reading simple patterns. Model how they are going to read the pattern. Use lines to represent a long note and dots to represent a short note. Move your hand below the lines and lift your hand when students should stop humming. See example below. Let them know you are the orchestra leader, so they must watch you for direction. Have students start with a basic "mmmmm" hum. Move onto humming different sounds, TAAAAA, AHHHHH, LAAAAAA, and so on.

Example: _____ · · ____ ____ · · · · __ __ _____

"mmmmmmm / m / m / mmm / mmm / m / m / m / m / mm / mm / mmmm"

Mirroring

Hold up a mirror. Talk to the students about what they see in a mirror and tell students they are going to pretend to be mirrors. Students work with partners. As they listen to music, one partner will move in time to the music as the other copies the movements. Instruct students to begin when you start the music. The students must listen to the style of the music and move accordingly. If it is a soft, light piece, they should move slowly and easily. If it is a jazzy piece, students change their style of movements. The person who is acting as the mirror must concentrate and follow his or her partner's movements. Have partners take turns being the mirror.

Easy-to-make Musical Instruments

Coffee Can Drums

Collect coffee or other cans without a top. Cut off the top of a balloon and stretch it across the top of the can. Secure with a rubber band around the rim. To play the drum students can use a pencil or their hands to beat the top of the drum, rub a pencil up and down the side of the can, or tap the metal bottom of the can.

Maracas

Take two yogurt or pudding cups. Place 10 to 20 dried beans or small pebbles in one of the cups and glue the openings of the cups together. Allow to dry. Reinforce the glue by taping the cups together with masking tape at the seam. Glue white paper to the outside of the cups to make a surface that can be decorated, or glue decorative wrapping paper around the cups. Add decorations if desired. Shake the maracas to make musical sounds.

Tambourine

Have each student decorate the bottoms of two paper plates. Staple the plates almost completely together along the outside rims of the plates, decorated sides out. Put a handful of beans inside the plates and finish stapling.

Rain Stick

Use a paper towel roll and close one end with tape and paper. Twist a small coat hanger so that it fits inside. Add a handful of rice or beans. Close the open end with tape and paper. Cover the entire paper towel roll with brown paper from a paper bag reinforcing the closures at the end. Decorate the rain stick to look like wood. You may find pliers or a wire cutter helpful for working with the hanger.

> **My message to the world is "Let's swing, sing, shout, make noise! Let's not mimic death before our time comes! Let's be wet and noisy."**
>
> —Mel Brooks, interview, New York Times, March 30, 1975

Color Wheel

Directions: Paint the color wheel using primary colors. Mix the primary colors to make secondary colors. See chart below:

1 = Red

2 = Orange (red + yellow)

3 = Yellow

4 = Green (yellow + blue)

5 = Blue

6 = Purple (blue + red)

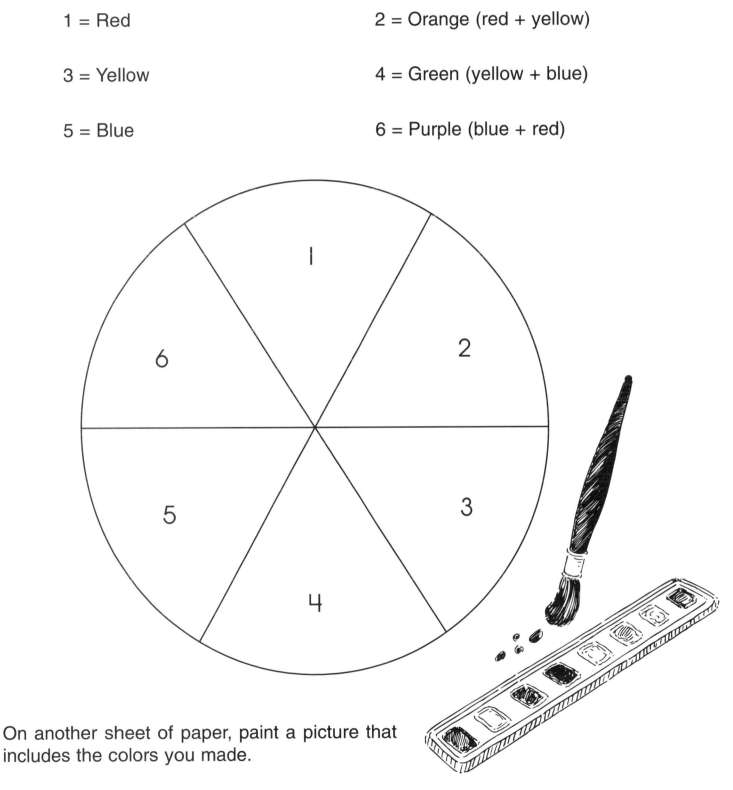

On another sheet of paper, paint a picture that includes the colors you made.

HOMEWORK IDEAS

Most schools and districts have a homework policy that outlines how much time should be spent on homework each night. If there is no policy, get a folder for each student and put his or her name or assigned number on it. Use a cover sheet which details the assignments for each day and includes a space for comments. Reading should be assigned nightly and recorded in a reading log.

As you are planning, decide what to include in the homework packets. Prepare the packets to send home on Monday and collect on Friday. The papers can be placed in the student folder. Pass the folders out to the students or distribute them to the student cubbies or mailboxes. Pick a location in the room where homework folders are to be returned on Fridays.

The goal of homework is to supplement, enrich, and reinforce skills. The homework should come from all of the different areas of the curriculum. Here are some interesting homework ideas.

- Write a creative story with spelling words.

- Find rhyming words for a given word.

- Write a letter to a pen pal.

- Go on a scavenger hunt for shapes or household items. Find things that are round, or shiny, or non-living, and so on.

- Word searches or crossword puzzles.

- Look for thermometers in the neighborhood. Where can they be found?

- Pretend you are a reporter. Interview someone you admire.

- Practice skip counting.

- Complete puzzles made from a Number Chart.

> Information provided by a teacher or textbook is generally, and wrongfully, perceived as knowledge....[Instead] knowledge is something created through a process of personal involvement that allows for complex relationships between the learners (including the teacher) and the text and the context of the classroom, even when the classroom includes the larger community . . . We should establish classrooms where children are encouraged to take responsibility for their learning, to become independent writers, readers, thinkers, and speakers, and to take an active role in creating a more just society.
>
> —Michael Hartoonian

Student _____   Week of _____

Teacher _____

Homework

Monday	Tuesday	Wednesday	Thursday

Teacher or Parent Comments

Parents: Read with your child 15 minutes every day. On the days you read with your child, initial the homework sheet.

Parent Signature _____   **Date** _____

Teacher: Use this form for your weekly homework assignments. Add your name and room number in the space provided. Fill in the assignment for each day. Note upcoming tests. Send this home with students on Monday with any homework sheets attached.

CHAPTER THREE: ORGANIZATION

PHYSICAL LAYOUT OF THE CLASSROOM

There are several important issues to consider before you set up your room. Are you going to use centers? Do you have desks or tables in your room for students? How do you want to arrange student desks—in groups, in rows, or individually? Do you know in advance if any of your students need wheelchair access, or an area where there is little visual distraction? What built-in features like chalkboards, shelves, windows, sinks will affect where you want students working?

Other important factors that will affect your decisions follow.

- All walkways and high traffic areas should be kept clear for safety. This includes doors, closets, and centers.

- Quiet areas such as the reading corner, the library, and the listening, writing, and poetry centers should be separated from noisy areas, such as blocks, math, or music.

- The art area should be near a sink for access to water for washing and clean up.

- Certain centers require electricity, such as the computer, the listening center, and the music center. The location of the electrical outlets could affect the location of these centers.

- If your classroom computer is going to be on-line, it will have to be close to the phone line.

- Your computer should be located as far as possible from dusty, sunny, and busy places.

- Have separate places in the room for large group activities, small group work, and individual desk areas.

- You will need places to store student work.

Draw an outline map of your classroom on a large piece of paper. Include any immovable and crucial objects on your classroom "map" such as doors, radiators, posts, electrical outlets, the chalkboard, windows, and bulletin boards. Use small pieces of paper to represent desks, filing cabinets, your computer(s), centers, bookshelves, and so on.

Note on the paper "furniture" any important things to keep in mind as you are arranging the room on paper such as *needs electricity.* Move things around on the map before you move a stick of furniture.

The desk arrangement you choose should be what works best for you. To facilitate cooperative groups, four or five students to a table cluster works nicely for a group Using this type of seating, you can assign a table monitor to pass out and collect papers.

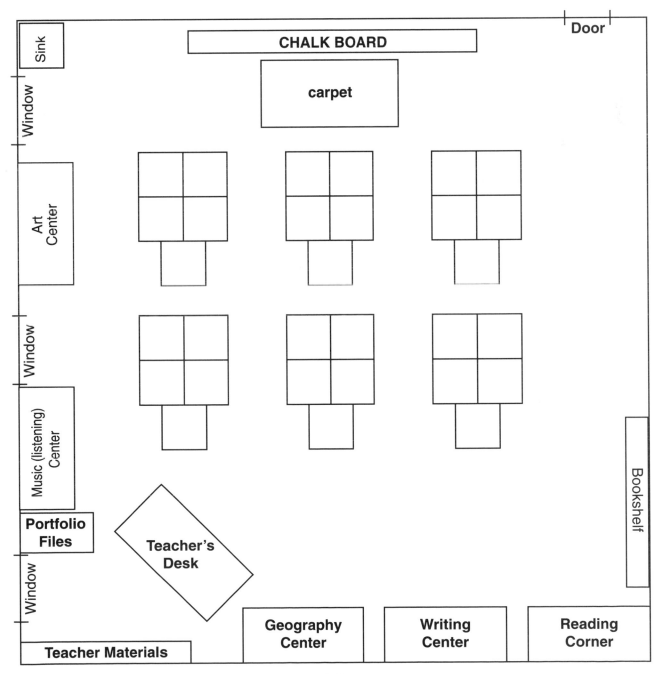

SCHEDULING

Following a daily schedule will make you more effective as a teacher. Schedules let the students know what is coming next, and keep you on track. To make a schedule, start by finding out what times may be planned for you already. Your school may have music, art, or science programs that regularly require students to be away from your classroom. Your principal may want to have all students who are in an English Language Development Program to be meeting at the same time. There are usually scheduled recess or lunch times. You may have scheduled yard, bus, or lunchroom duties.

Once you know when students will be with you, divide the day into blocks of time for each subject. Opportunities to read, write, and work with mathematics should occur every day. Your school or district may have requirements about the minimal amount of time that should be devoted to certain subjects. If you have an assistant, consider how you will use him or her during the time assigned to you.

Many teachers write their schedule on a posterboard and post it in the class. Other prefer to write it on the board with daily updates, so that students get in the habit of consulting it every day. If you choose to write the schedule every day, writing it can become a student job. Second-grade students love to write "official" signs.

Daily Schedule
School Day
8:00 - 2:30

8:00	Entry Task
8:15	Opening and Community Time
8:50	Math
9:30	Recess
9:45	Reading *Full Group Instruction* or *Guided Reading* or *Independent Work* or *Centers*
10:55	Spelling/Phonics
11:10	Lunch
11:55	Shared Oral Reading
12:10	M, W Writer's Workshop T, Th Science or Social Studies F Art
1:15	Recess
1:25	M, W, F Physical Education T, Th Writing and Music
2:10	Closing
2:30	Dismissal

CLASSROOM ROUTINES

Entry Tasks

Frequently students arrive at school after being rushed every moment since they were awakened. Start the day with an entry task which allows students time to make the transition from home, morning care, or school bus to school.

Post a different task every day. Suggested entry tasks are journal entries in science, writing, personal, or math journals, or Sustained Silent Reading (See description of SSR on page 18). When students arrive, they check the task notice, put their things away, get what they need for the entry task, and begin to work at their own paces. The entry task helps the students settle and focus, and gives you some time for last-minute preparations or to handle any last-minute crisis.

THE OPENING AND COMMUNITY TIME

This is an important activity in the day. It is the first time when you and your students are meeting as a community in the day. Establish a regular routine for the Opening. Possible activities for the opening include a flag salute, taking attendance, reviewing and updating the calendar, reviewing the days of the week and time, a community meeting, introducing theme activities, and a presentation of activities planned for the day. Interact with and observe your students as you go through the activities. You will quickly learn to spot who is having a hard day and may need some encouragement to get on track.

Closing

Use the last fifteen minutes of the day to bring your class back together for a group seated activity. You can use this time to summarize the day with a closing activity like the Activity Review Cards described below, to review the homework assignment for the evening, to remind students of any special events of the next day, or to pass out special recognitions you would like to give. Your students will benefit by having a few moments of mental regrouping before they have to go home, go to day care, or get on a bus. You will benefit by taking an opportunity to assess the instructional day with your students and having a relatively calm end of the day.

Activity Review Cards

As part of your closing activities, review the lessons and activities of the day as a group. As students recount what happened during the day, you write it onto a 5" x 7" index card with the day's date at the top. When finished, you all read the card aloud. Display the index cards in a calendar-like display, adding to the display for the month. At the end of the month bind the cards into a class book for the classroom library, and prepare for the next month's activity review. You will all enjoy rereading the activity books at different points in the year. An additional benefit is that you will have an instant assessment of what parts of your instructional day were most effective.

TRANSITIONS

Any time you change activities you present your students with problems to solve. They need to stop what they are doing, put it away, and move to the next activity. For some students this is a challenge. You will notice that most students are not their quietest while in transition. You can reduce the stress of transition time by having reasonable expectations of your students, and explaining what the expectations are in advance. First you need to get their attention.

Signals

Many teachers pick a signal to attract students attention. Commonly used signals include ringing a small bell, turning out the lights, clapping, or holding one hand in the air. Once you use your signal, do not give any instructions until you have the attention of all your students. Once you have their attention, give them the following information.

- Explain what is going to happen.

- Indicate how they will move, such as form a line or walk across the room.

- Tell them where they are going.

- Inform them what they will be doing.

Moving students from place to place, either within a classroom or from the classroom to another location at the school, can be tricky. Some schools require that students move from place to place in single file, while other schools do not. If you are new to your school, ask colleagues to tell you what your school culture is.

71

> **Student achievement can be interpreted only in light of the quality of the program they experience.**
>
> —National Science Education Standards, 1996

RECORD KEEPING

One of the keys to a successful classroom is being organized. Know what records your school requires, and what records your teaching plans require. Records you may need to keep include daily attendance records, assessment records (including portfolios and test results), lesson plans, permanent school records (usually kept at the school), homework tracking, and reading logs. Plan your record keeping as soon as you know you have a class.

Give Each Student a Number

When you get your first class list, assign each student a number. Students place this number on all of their work next to their name. When checking for missing work, put the work in numerical order and scan the numbers to find who has turned in work. The numbers can also be used to count off when lining up or collecting work. The number system is particularly useful if your class size changes a lot during the year. You just give new students the next number or reassign a number belonging to a former student who has moved.

Daily Attendance

An attendance record book is extremely useful. Its obvious purpose is keeping track of attendance, but it has other uses as well. Update this book every day, and keep it close to the classroom exit where it is easy to grab in an emergency. In the event of a fire, earthquake, or other disaster, you need to be able to call roll and check and see that each student is accounted for. If something has happened to prevent you from calling roll, the person in charge of your class will need the information.

Even if your school or district provides computerized attendance sheets, keeping personal records is extremely useful for parent conferences and tracking patterns of absences that may be red flags to other problems the student is facing or help explain poor performance in the class.

Grade Book

You will need a grade book. List students' names in alphabetical order. If you have space on the page, leave some blank lines between student names so that you can add new students in alphabetical order when they join your class. Assign different pages in the grade book to different subjects. Ask for a copy of the report card you must fill out for each student, so that you know what information you must report, and therefore must have records of. You will be using different assessment criteria for different types of work. Label sections for homework, projects and reports, and tests.

Record grades daily or weekly. Try to keep the paper flowing through your room so you don't drown in it. As you record grades, include information on the grade book that will help you identify the source of the grade when it comes time to do progress reports. For example, in the spelling section you might note at the top of a column of test results, the date of the test and the total number of questions or words included on the test. In a social studies section you might note the name of the project graded and include a column for a content grade, a column for the mechanics grade, and an overall grade. There are computer programs commercially available that make the record-keeping process even easier. Grade Pro and Teacher's Toolbox are two of them.

ASSESSMENT

Assessment is an on-going process. You will use several different means of assessment for your students that will include portfolios, rubrics, tests, quizzes, and anecdotal records. You will be evaluating daily work, projects, class participation, tests, and homework.

Portfolios

A portfolio is a collection of a student's work in each subject area that reflects the student's abilities. Keep both formal and informal portfolios for each student. Involve your students in selecting work to be kept in these files. Portfolios are the most useful tool for recognizing conceptual growth and to see the changes that the student is making throughout the school year.

Rubrics

Rubrics are used to evaluate student work. Establish criteria you will judge student work against. Assign different number values to each tier of your rubric. Let your students know in advance what the criteria is for the project. Students also benefit greatly by helping to develop the rubric for a project.

Tests and Other Numeric Grades

As you grade papers on which you are giving only a numeric grade (objective tests and papers where there is only one right answer) make a note of the number of correct answers the students make in the grade book. Remember to make a note of the total number of questions you are asking each time.

Anecdotal Records

Prepare a notebook in which you collect notes and observations about your students. Dedicate a page or section to each student. As you work with students during the day, take notes of anything interesting you observe. Date all entries. Include a record of reading that you do with each student at least once a week.

> ### TIP!
> Make a card chart with a card for each student. When a student arrives, he or she pulls his or her attendance card. A quick glance lets you know who is present.

A quick way to take notes without carrying around a big folder is to carry several sheets of self-adhesive file folder or address labels on a clipboard. As you notice something, write the student's name on the top of the label, add the date, and note what you want to remember. At the end of the day transfer the self-adhesive sheets to your anecdotal records.

Writer's Workshop Rubric

on a four-point scale, 4 being the highest

4- Well thought-out and complete work, editing and revision done.

3- Story frame in place

2- Needs to develop story

1- Started topic

Math Rubric

on a four-point scale, 4 being the highest

4- Compete answer, shows understanding of concept

3- Correct answer, did not show thinking

2- Has some idea of the topic, not clear

1- Does not understand concept

73

> Never discourage anyone...who continually makes progress, no matter how slow.
>
> —Plato

Record Sheets

In addition to anecdotal records, you will want to track who is turning in homework on time. Make a place in your grade book for this information and keep it updated.

REPORT CARDS

Gather Your Records

As you figure grades for report cards, you will want to use your best judgment about what work should be reflected in the final grade, and what can be given greater or lesser importance. Before you sit down to write your report cards, gather all relevant material—portfolios, your grade book, and anecdotal records. Expect to spend a week or two doing report cards.

Make a Rough Draft

Some schools and districts provide preprinted report card forms that you fill in. Others will provide you with blank forms on which to write grades by hand that become the permanent report card. Make copies of your blank forms—one for each student. You can compile your records on this sheet, and any mistakes you make (and you will make some) can be entered correctly in the final copy.

Some examples of mathematics assessment

- Observation
- Interviews and questions
- Student writing and journals
- Open-ended question responses
- Class participation and performance

Some examples of on-going assessment in language arts

- classroom discussions
- one-on-one conferences with students
- student participation
- teacher-designed questions
- student's ability to read aloud

Figuring Grades

What are the important grades to include in this reporting period? Some schools and districts will mandate reporting. Others will leave it to your professional judgment. Is every grade as important as the others?

Some teachers like to drop the worst grade from the student's work and then average the rest of the grades. Others like to give different weights to student work based on its importance.

Example of Weighting Grades

For example, Johanna, the second-grade teacher, needs to calculate a science grade for Lita Brown. The assignments and grades she has recorded for Lita are the following.

In-class project
raising and observing a plant
Total possible points - 5
Grade—5 or 100%

Homework assignment
gathering different seeds and comparing them
Total possible points - 4
Grade—4 or 100%

Keeping a discovery journal
Lita wrote in the journal extensively every day.

Two in-class science tests
Grade—7/10 (7 correct of 10) or 70% and
Grade—6/9 (6 correct of 9) or 67%

You can see that Lita's exploration and discovery work is excellent as reflected in the grades. She doesn't do as well on tests.

Lita participates actively in class.

Johanna could decide that the discovery and exploration aspects of the curriculum are worth 75% of the grade, tests will be worth 15%, and class participation 10%.

She will figure Lita's grade by adding the exploration and discovery aspects together. She then averages the grades by dividing the total by the number of items included in the total.

Plant project	100
Seed homework	100
Journal	100
Total is	300/3= 100%

Since 75 is the value for exploration and discovery, then 100% of 75 = 75 or [75 x 1.0] As she has 100% in the discovery part of the grade, she will receive the full 75 points of the grade.

Test 1	70%
Test 2	67%
Total is	137%/2 = 69%

Since 15 is the value for tests, then 69 % of 15 = 10 [15 x 1.69]. She would receive 10 points of a possible 15 for her tests.

She participates actively in class, so Johanna will give her the full 10 points for class participation.

Lita's total grade is therefore 75 + 10 + 10 = 95.

You can weight your grading system to reflect your curricular goals. Once you have made a decision, treat all students the same way. Make a note of your grade formula for future reference.

Report Card Comments

Many report cards have sections for teacher comments. Draft your comments on a separate sheet of paper before you write them on the final document. Edit your comments for content and mechanical errors. Use a positive tone when writing report cards. Your words will be remembered for many years.

PERMANENT RECORDS

Most schools and districts have a permanent record that is maintained for each student throughout the child's school experience. Check with your principal or other teachers about what information you are required to complete for each student.

This document is used as a reference by future teachers of the student and other school personnel. It can also be consulted by parents. It is generally a good idea to word any information written in this document with a positive or a neutral tone, and to avoid irrelevant opinions.

STANDARDIZED TESTS

Standardized tests are a fact of scholastic life. Try to make standardized testing as positive an experience as you can.

Tell students to take their time and check their work. When they are not sure of an answer, they should try to pick the best answer. Teach them some test-taking strategies. A good source of test-taking strategies for second-graders is the Frank Schaffer book *Test-Taking Skills Grade 2*.

Testing can be stressful for students. Try to schedule a fun, non-structured activity to follow testing, such as drawing, working on puzzles, games. Young students need to move around and standardized testing does not provide for this.

Communicating with Caretakers About Testing

Send a note home to parents and caretakers letting them know when the standardized testing is taking place. Remind parents of these simple guidelines to follow.

- Students need plenty of sleep.

- A healthy breakfast starts the day off right.

- Get student to school on time.

- Try to avoid any absences that can be rescheduled such as doctor's appointments.

Preparing for Standardized Tests

Math

In the math section, many items are on a page. It is easy for a student to lose his or her place or look at the wrong picture for the problem. Have the students use sheets of colored construction paper (4-1/4" x 5-1/2") to mark their places on the test.

Reading comprehension

The readings may be long and include many passages. Provide your students with lots of experience reading long passages in the course of the school year. Make packets of varying length sample readings with questions for your students to practice.

Spelling

Many of the spelling items on the tests are tricky. There is frequent use of words that are not spelled phonetically. Teach your students to ask themselves, "What looks right?"

Testing Terms You Should Know

- Mean Raw Score = Average score for your class

- Mean Scaled Scores = The national average score for all students taking the test.

- National PR-S = Percentile Rank and Stanine Score for your students on a particular test. A stanine score is like a percentile, but it is broken into nine levels instead of 100.

- 1-3 = below average

- 4-6 = average

- 7-10 = above average

CHAPTER FOUR RELATIONSHIPS

SOCIAL ORDER OF THE ROOM

Rules

Rules in a classroom help you define your expectations of your students, and help students understand your expectations. Rules should be stated positively and should be easy to enforce. You don't need to restate school rules as your classroom rules. Following school rules is understood and expected.

Start the year by writing classroom rules together. Create a chart to remind students about the rules and add appropriate graphics. When discussing rules, discuss consequences for breaking rules.

Sample Classroom Rules

Raise your hand to talk.

Keep hands, feet, and objects to yourself.

Listen when others are speaking.

Follow directions the first time they are given.

Sample Consequences

First Infraction—Verbal Warning

Second Infraction—Lose recess

Third Infraction—Note or call home

Fourth Infraction—See the principal

Managing Classroom Behavior

- Give clear directions.

- Be consistent in enforcing classroom rules and consequences.

- Use a calm approach and remain as neutral as possible.

- Never allow a student to physically harm anyone.

- Have an immediate consequence for rule violations.

- Remind the student of the rules if it looks like he or she is about to break one.

Conflict Resolution

Teach students to be their own problem solvers. Model conflict resolution behaviors. When two students are having a conflict, you might ask them, "What can you do to solve this problem?" or advise students to use their words to explain how they feel.

If students cannot verbalize their feelings on their own, you can help them identify their emotions. Many times children do not have the vocabulary to express their feelings, and their feelings are strong and confusing. Include other students in arriving at a solution to resolve the conflict by discussing the issues that brought about the conflict.

> **TIP!**
>
> *Model the behavior you expect from your students.*
> - *Arrive on time or early.*
> - *Be prepared.*
> - *Expect to have a great day.*

Classroom Meetings

Solve disputes or talk about problems at a classroom meeting. This democratic approach allows each person in the classroom share his or her feelings in a non-threatening atmosphere. You can lead the discussion or appoint a student to do so. Establish ground rules for discussion such as each person is allowed to say his or her piece and that the solution reached must be agreeable to the whole class.

Positive Reinforcement

Recognizing behavior you want to encourage in your classroom is a more effective way to encourage your students to act appropriately than recognizing unacceptable behavior.

Tape a 3" by 5" index card on each student's desk. When you catch someone doing a good job, place a mark on his or her card. The mark could be a happy face, a star, a sticker, or a stamp. Follow making the mark with a brief comment about their behavior. For example, "I like how you are reading." When you recognize a student for doing something well, the student feels proud and you have alerted the rest of the students about behavior that you value.

When a student accumulates 20 marks on the card, he or she can exchange it for a classroom privilege. Decide upon what the privileges will be as a class. The privileges might be a pass to use the computer, helping the teacher, being first in line, or sitting at the teacher's desk.

Unity Builders

These are cooperative projects such as class quilts, posters with a certain theme topic, and group art. A class puzzle is a great way to show how each person is an important part of the class. Cut as many puzzle pieces as you have students. Students decorate their pieces and sign their names. Work together to assemble the puzzle. Each student is a part of the whole class, just like each puzzle piece is a part of the puzzle.

STARTING THE YEAR

Here are some simple ideas that can help get your started on the right track

Calendar

Keep a monthly calendar at your desk. Use it to keep track of special events, assemblies, fire drills, special events, and when report cards are due. Keeping all this information recorded and in one place makes planning and organization a lot easier. Remember to add this information to your plan book.

Paper Tide

Centralize the locations where you keep unmarked and unreviewed papers and papers ready to return to students. Have an "In-box" where students turn in work when they have finished the assignments so that all of the papers you need to look over and correct are in one place. Place an "Out-box" for corrected work that has been entered in your grade book and that needs to be passed back to students.

Cubbies for Kids

Individual cubbies (or cubicles) are ideal to use as a distribution center for your students. Cubbies make distributing communications a lot easier. If your classroom does not have cubbies, consider acquiring individual letter/paper trays.

Supplies

Label all classroom storage and supplies. Make sure that all materials to be used are organized and accessible. Go over where the supplies are stored so that everyone in the classroom knows where they are and how to keep them in order. Have students take responsibility for putting the supplies away.

> **Taking an interest in what students are thinking and doing is often a much more powerful form of encouragement than praise.**
>
> —Robert Martin

Getting to Know Your School Culture and Community

Many people comprise the school. Getting to know each one can be a difficult task, however it is well worth it. Knowing the people to whom you can go for support makes life at school easier.

Principal

Usually the principal of a school is a former teacher who has gone to school to get an administrative credential. In many schools and districts the principal is the person who hires you at a school, while the school or district employs you. The principal is your manager. He or she is accountable to the powers-that-be and to parents for what occurs in your classroom. Some principals spend a lot of time being educational leaders—keeping in touch with teachers and students, spending time in the classroom and in community areas like the playground or the lunchroom. Other principals focus their energies on running the business side of the school. Their jobs are defined in part by the system in which they work.

As your manager, your principal will observe your work in the classroom. He or she may make an appointment with you to see a lesson or may drop in to see what you do in the classroom. Formal and informal observations may be noted in your personnel file. If you have a good relationship with your principal, the observations can be a learning experience for you.

You will want to communicate well with the principal. To communicate well, you must share your frustrations and your successes. When you have questions or difficulty dealing with a parent, part of the principal's job is to support you. Don't forget to share your successes with your principal. He or she will be happy to hear those, too!

Buddy Teacher

Find a teacher at your grade level who you feel comfortable asking everyday questions about anything. A buddy teacher will let you know about school culture. Questions will come up about core literature books, curriculum planning, field trips, assemblies, and more, that are specific to your grade level. A buddy teacher might just have the answer to your question.

Colleagues

On one hand teaching is isolating. You spend most of your days with people much younger than you are, and frequently you will feel alone dealing with the challenges in your classroom, because you are alone. You can alleviate this feeling by getting to know the people with whom you work. Many schools have an area where you can eat lunch or meet with other teachers. Find common interests to discuss instead of work. Frequently teachers at a school will have a social committee to plan gatherings and special events. Try to participate in as many as possible. A natural outgrowth of the friendships you build is a support system.

> Teaching is a moral calling, a craft, and an intellectual occupation. It is often values that bring one to education in the first place. The craft develops through experience and reflection upon that experience. What is hardest to maintain in the midst of the immediate demands of the classroom is the intellectual aspect of teaching, which, though less apparent on an everyday level than the craft issues, still pervades and underlies every good teacher's practice. It has to do with teachers' analysis of how children learn, of the role of ethnicity, gender, and class in learning, of the relationship between school and society, and of the translation of moral values into specific classroom practice.
>
> —Herbert Kohl

Custodian

Get to know the custodians of the school. They know where everything is. When you need furniture, special cleaning tools, light bulbs, and paper towels, talk to the custodians. They are powerful. Teach students to be responsible for cleaning the classroom at the end of each day. This will make the custodian's job a lot easier, and create an ally for you. There will come the day when your students have had a big party, you have all been painting, and several students drop paint water on the floor, and you will need special help cleaning.

Know how to request supplies such as tissues and paper towels. Learn how to request repairs, verbally or in writing if you need them. Sometimes you need to submit a work order through the office.

Resource Teachers

Many schools have teachers who do not have their own classrooms. They may provide special services such as a reading laboratory, coordinate the art or music program, or manage the instructional materials owned by the school. Frequently resource teachers will be able to answer questions or make suggestions about educational and classroom management issues. In some schools where the principal is extremely busy, the resource teacher is the first person you ask for educational program support.

Resource Center Some school districts maintain centralized resource centers for teachers where you may have access to free photocopying services, district-created educational materials. The principal or resource teacher will know whether such a place exists, where it is, and how to use it.

Librarian

The school librarian can be another strong resource for you. Frequently school libraries have a regularly scheduled time when your students will go the library to learn about the resources there, to enjoy literacy activities, to read, and to check out books. The school librarian knows what books are in the library and can help you find literature and non-fiction that will support your educational program.

Office Manager

The people who run the office keep the school moving. This is a tremendous job. Every piece of paper that comes to the school goes through the office. Attendance, payroll, mail, bulletins, field trip requests, book orders, and all official outward bound papers are all handled by the front office. Ask questions and get familiar with the procedures. Find out about deadlines for field trip request, district mail, and other information from the front office.

Supply Manager

Learn what supplies are available on site and how to order them. Sometimes you will need to place an order well in advance. While you are planning, make a list of supplies you will need. Place your order in time to get the supplies and materials you need for your classroom.

School Nurse

Many schools and districts have a school nurse full- or part-time. The nurse will coordinate hearing and vision screenings, keep medical information on students with health problems, and often has an office with beds where students who have taken ill may lie down. If you are concerned about a student's health, consult the nurse. He or she may also be able to help you find resources to assist the families of your students who need health care services.

PTA

The PTA is an organization of parents and teachers united to work together to improve the school. The PTA is different in every school. Some are active, some are not. Some will want you to be active in their organization, some will not. Most PTAs raise funds for special projects that the school has identified as necessary or wanted. Find out what activities the PTA handles at your school. They may have a project that interests you or could directly benefit your class.

The Teacher's Union

Many public school district teachers are represented by a union. Usually there will be at least one union representative at your school. Particularly in a large district, a union representative can be helpful in learning who you have to speak to for help in employment issues.

HOME/SCHOOL CONNECTION

There are many ways to make a connection between home and school. The best way to do this is through communication. This can range from notes home to a monthly newsletter.

Send home corrected work with comments so that the parents can see what their child is working on in class and how he or she is doing. Homework that requires adult contributions is another way to connect with the parents and help them be involved in the educational process.

Telephone calls are also useful. You can talk with parents at length and get a sense of what the home environment is like. Use the phone as a way to communicate any special concerns to the parent. Use the phone at least once a week to call a parent to compliment one of your students. The parents will love to hear good news from you, and they won't dread your calls.

We are going to have to find ways of organizing ourselves cooperatively, sanely, scientifically, harmonically and in regenerative spontaneity with the rest of humanity around earth . . . We are not going to be able to operate our spaceship earth successfully nor for much longer unless we see it as a whole spaceship and our fate as common. It has to be everybody or nobody.

—Buckminster Fuller

Back-to-School Night

Back-to-School Night usually occurs within the first six weeks of school. Prepare in advance. This is your opportunity to let parents know what is going to happen in the upcoming academic year, to find out what questions they have, and how they can be involved in the instructional program.

Make an information packet to hand out to parents that includes the following.

- Welcome letter

- Your background

- List of supplies that students need

- The rules and consequences of breaking the rules

- School policy on absences and discipline

- Grading policies—yours and the school's

- Report card schedule and basis of your evaluations

- Homework procedures and policies

- Field trip information

- A wish list—often parents want to provide materials that you can use with their children such as disposable cameras, film processing, computer programs, materials for your centers or for special art projects, and specific books

- Any other information that you want parents to know or you think they might want to know

On Back-to-School night, go through the packet with parents. Try to make it as comfortable and informal as possible so that the parents will ask questions and you can get to know each other. Answer any questions that come up as you are talking about policies. Briefly talk about the curriculum that will be covered during the year so that they can get a feel about what second grade is like.

I always tell parents that our job in second grade is to continue to refine the skills the students have brought with them and to bring out the students' curiosity and creativity. Display the curricular programs your school has adopted and talk briefly about them. Give parents an opportunity to look over the materials. Set out the teacher's guides, so that parents can see exactly what you will be doing. Many of the new math programs written to National Teachers of Mathematics Standards will be new to your parents, as is the emphasis on thinking strategies rather than drill and memorization. You could even demonstrate a lesson and have the parents participate.

Parent/Teacher Conference

Parent/Teacher conferences usually occur midway into the second quarter of the school year. You meet personally with parents or caretakers of every one of your students to talk about the student's academic and social progress. Many teachers like to have the classroom filled with student work during conferences as it makes the students feel proud, and it gives parents an idea of what second-grade work looks like.

Generally the school or district has days set aside specifically for conferences, and specific guidelines about the minimal length of the conference. Frequently your in-class time with your students will be shorter on conference days. Usually you will be expected to put together the schedule of which parents you will see when. Some teachers like to assign times to parents without consulting the parents first, other teachers like to give parents the option to choose a "best time" and then juggle the schedule.

Your school may have specific notices you are required to send out. Others let you send whatever notice you want, as long as you send one out. Your school may provide you with a schedule of times to fill in with the names of parents who are coming, and when they are coming. Send reminder notices of the scheduled meeting the day before you are to meet. Include your school phone number.

Post the schedule outside your door, and place a few chairs outside where parents can sit while they are waiting for you. Leave your door open so that the parents with whom you are talking will only stay for their allotted time. When they hear the next parents arrive, they will know that their time is almost up. Decide how inflexible you are going to be about your schedule—if a parent comes late, will you ask him or her to leave when the time is up, or will you run behind schedule a bit? Check with other teachers to see what they will be doing with late parents.

Prepare for your conference in advance. Outline the information you want to cover about each child so that when parents are there, you can remember all the important information. Group papers, portfolios, and files pertaining to each student and have them at hand when the parents walk through the door. You want to make the best use of the short time you have with the parents.

During the conference, put parents at ease by sharing a table. You may intimidate them if you sit at your desk while they are at a table or a child-sized desk. Many schools and districts require you to turn in a sheet signed by the parents who have visited you. Ask them to sign this before you start the conference.

Always start saying something positive. Refer to your outline during the conference. Take notes of parent comments directly on your outline. File the outline as a benchmark against which to monitor the student's progress throughout the year. Provide the parents with a copy to take home with them if your school does not have a standardized form you are supposed to use.

Talk with parents during the conference, not at them. Remember, you are talking about their child. They know the child best, ask for their insights. Listen to the parents' concerns. Show them work samples and portfolio pieces to give them a picture of how their student is doing. They will be able to put the work in context if you have decorated the room with a variety of student work. Open the lines of communication. The parents, the student, and you are a team. The goal is for the student to succeed in school. Everyone wants the student to have a productive and enjoyable second-grade year.

Open House

Open House generally occurs within two months of the end of school. It is a showcase of the students' accomplishments during the school year. Display class big books, writer's workshop books, math projects, science discoveries, and other class projects.

The week before Open House have students create an invitation to the event which they take home to their parents. This acts as a reminder and also as a way to practice your student's skills. Have students follow proper friendly letter format, include two reasons why students believe their parents should attend the open house, and end with a closing statement.

Prepare for the visit by having each student prepare and decorate two folders from construction paper. One folder will store work that must stay in school and the other folder is for the parents to take home.

Have students design a tour of the classroom for their parents. Decide what centers they want to show their parents. Have students prepare a demonstration of a favorite group activity.

CLASSROOM VOLUNTEERS

Classroom volunteers can be parents, members of the community, high school students, or students from an upper grade at your school.

When you know that you will have volunteer help in your classroom, think in advance about the kinds of jobs you want help with. Have supplies and easy-to-follow instructions available.

Sometimes the kind of help you can expect will depend on the age and maturity of the volunteer. Older students will enjoy helping you compile homework packets, organizing shelves and closets, doing certain kinds of cleaning, sharpening pencils, and cutting materials. Adults will usually be happy helping in these ways also, but you may

want to use them to give individual help to students or to word process student writings. All volunteers can listen and work with young readers. Volunteers can also help keep a supervisory eye on a messy art center. Your volunteers may have a specific job they wish to do.

Make the volunteers feel like a part of your class. Introduce volunteers to your class by name as you welcome them. Let the students know that the volunteers are to be treated with respect. Thank the volunteers for coming, both verbally and in writing.

Have a sign-in sheet by the door to keep track of the volunteers who come into your classroom. You'll be sure to remember who gets a thank-you card.

Set aside a table or workspace in your classroom for volunteers where volunteers can work. Use the form on page 86 to communicate with your volunteers. List what needs to be done and leave it at the workspace. Use your volunteers to free you for as much teaching as you can.

Welcome all the help that you can get, you will need it!

Volunteer Information

Name: _____

Address: _____

Phone: _____

Days and Times Available: _____

_____

What kind of work would you prefer to do in the classroom? _____

_____

_____

Do you have a special talent you'd like to share with us? What is it? _____

_____

_____

_____

_____

_____

_____

Use the back of this form if you need more space

Thanks for helping today

Date

Projects for Volunteer:

CHAPTER FIVE: CLOSING THOUGHTS

ENGLISH LANGUAGE DEVELOPMENT

You may have students in your class who do not speak English as a first language. In schools where there are many students who speak languages other than English as a first language, you will probably have access to an English Language Development program with guidelines for its use outlined by your school or district. Remember learning a language is a process. It took you years to speak English well, and you were able to concentrate most of your language development on one language.

If you find yourself with a small group of non-English speaking students in your class, and you have no administrative support, check your school's resource room, local university library, or Internet resources for some specific plans and courses of study to assist the students. Some quick guidelines include providing picture cues for certain activities. Teach students the names of activities and materials (in the context of doing the activity) so that when they hear or see those words they will know what books or materials they need.

Assign the students peer mentors who can help them learn classroom vocabulary. When you change activities, take a moment to approach your non-English speaking students, look at them, and speak at a slower rate using a simple language structure with instructions. Model appropriate responses to questions.

Special Education Terms

Mainstreaming means placing a student with disabilities in a regular education classroom.

IDEA—*Individuals with Disabilities Education Act,* passed in 1990.

IDEA guarantees a student with disabilities the right to a free and appropriate education in the least restrictive environment, with maximum support of mainstreaming. Special classes are used only when appropriate to meet the needs of the individual student.

Least Restrictive Environment is the general education classroom setting.

Most Restrictive Environment is complete removal from mainstream society, such as an institution or hospital setting.

IEP means the *Individualized Education Program* required for each student receiving special education.

Your non-English speaking students also come from cultures where acceptable body language differs from what you may be used to. Perhaps as a child you were raised to look at an adult when the adult was talking to you. Looking away was disrespectful. Many cultures consider a child who looks an adult in the face insolent and defiant, so a well-mannered child will never look at an adult directly. Increase your level of awareness of the body language of these students.

Include the students in activities. Model respect for their culture and their intelligence to the class. Set the tone for acceptance of these students in your class. Your students will follow you. What to you may be little acts of kindness, may shine out as beacons of goodwill and inspiration to the student struggling to understand a new language and a new culture.

MAINSTREAMING

The IEP team meets annually to discuss goals and objectives and to make sure that progress is being made. If you are the teacher of a student on an IEP, you are responsible for implementing the curriculum to fulfill the goals and objectives.

However, you are not in this alone. Members of the IEP team should work closely with you. Help is available if you ask. Team members include the school nurse, the special education teacher, the school psychologist, a behavioral consultant, an occupational therapist, a special education supervisor, and other school personnel.

Seeking Speech Evaluations

By second grade most children have acquired accuracy in pronouncing most sounds. During second grade when a student demonstrates language articulation difficulties, an immediate speech evaluation is recommended to decide whether remediation is needed

ABSENCES

When A Student Is Absent

When a student is absent he or she can miss a lot of class work. Place a folder on his or her desk or cubbie labeled "Work Done in Your Absence." Throughout the day add papers and information to the folder. At the end of the day slip the folder into a resealable plastic bag decorated to make it look inviting and leave it for the student. Add to it each day the student is absent.

You can foster more personal responsibility in the class if you assign a student or team of two students to gather the materials an absent student will need to catch up. Call them the mentors. The mentors are also responsible for going through the package with the student who returns to explain any information that needs to be discussed.

Reproduce the sheet on page 91 to organize the information needed.

When You are Absent

Even if you have enjoyed perfect health before you started working as a teacher, you will get sick. You are exposed to lots of germs in a school. Usually by your third year of teaching your immunity is built enough so that you don't catch every cold or other virus that walks through your classroom door.

In addition, in-service educational experiences may be scheduled during the school day so that you must be away from your classroom.

Your school or district may have a service that arranges for substitutes or you may have to find your own. At the beginning of the year, find out what you need to do by asking another teacher or the school secretary.

If you are able, leave plans for the person substitute teaching in your stead. Use the form on page 92 to communicate with your "sub."

TEACHER-TO-TEACHER ADVICE

Child Abuse

In many states teachers are required by law to report any suspicion of child abuse. Proving abuse is not your responsibility, but reporting suspicions of abuse is. Some schools will follow up a teacher's suspicions, other schools require the teacher to act alone. Check with your school or district about your legal responsibilities.

Noise

Your classroom may get a little loud from time to time. When you recognize productive noise, you are hearing second graders learning. Learning is a social process. We want students to interact, ask questions, and have fun while they are learning.

Attitude is Everything

Sometimes just getting through one day seems like a struggle. You get up late, the drive to school is treacherous due to inclement weather, the students have to stay inside all day, a major sugar-related holiday is close-at-hand, you forgot you had lunchroom duty, the principal is going to observe your teaching, and when you get to school you discover you put on two different-colored socks. Days like these will happen. Things aren't always going to go the way you planned. This is okay. It is good to prepare some fun and enjoyable activities that involve a lot of laughing to use on a challenging day. Incorporate them into your instructional day when you need to lighten the atmosphere. Whether you stay with your original daily plans or wing an activity, try to make the best of your choice. There are teachable moments in everything that you do.

Personality—Let Yours Shine!

Great teachers can also be artists, musicians, multiple-language speakers, writers, athletes, community activists, or any of a number of talented people outside of the classroom. We must remember to bring our talents to school. I will always remember what my yard-duty partner, Carol Varner, told me just days before she retired after over 30 years of teaching. She said that if she hadn't been able to do art and music in class, she wouldn't have wanted to be a teacher.

I love music. When I do music with my students, I come alive. My students can feel that energy, and they respond to it. It fosters the learning environment of my classroom.

Remember to bring your personality into the classroom. Not only will you enjoy your job more, but your students will benefit as well.

Every second we live is a new and unique moment of the universe, a moment that never was before and never will be again. And what do we teach our children in school? We teach them that 2 and 2 makes 4 and that Paris is the capital of France. When will we also teach them what they are? We should say to each of them: Do you know what you are? You are a marvel. You are unique. In all the world there is no other child exactly like you. In the millions of years that have passed there has never been a child like you. And look at your body what a wonder it is! Your legs, your arms, your cunning fingers, the way you move! You may become a Shakespeare, a Michelangelo, a Beethoven. You have the capacity for anything. Yes, you are a marvel. And when you grow up can you then harm another who is, like you, a marvel? You must cherish one another. You must work—we must all work—to make this world worthy of its children.

—Pablo Casals

Take Care of Yourself

Teaching is a consuming job. It is easy to find yourself spending every waking minute thinking about your students, your classroom, and what you are going to do next, and every sleeping minute dreaming about school. There will be days when you are working ten or more hours just to keep up with your job responsibilities. This is a quick way to burn out. Pace yourself. Make yourself leave school after you have worked eight hours. Give yourself at least one weekend day for recreation - no schoolwork! Exercise regularly and take some classes that are not related to the field of education. Keep your life in balance, and you will be the most effective teacher you can be.

Name _____ **Date** _____

Welcome back! We missed you!

While you were gone we did the following projects.

_____

_____

_____

_____

_____

_____

Please turn these in by: _____

If you have any questions, ask me, or _____.

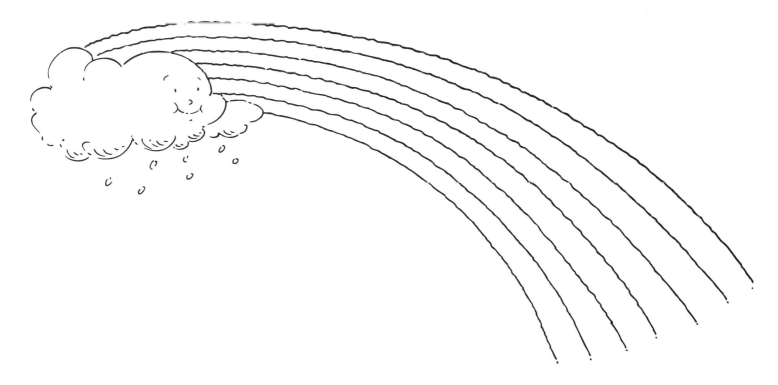

SUBSTITUTE INFORMATION SHEET

Daily Schedule: Special Instructions:

Include the time school starts, recess, lunch, and dismissal procedures as well as any special events that are taking place.

8:00 _____   _____

9:00 _____   _____

10:00 _____   _____

11:00 _____   _____

12:00 _____   _____

1:00 _____   _____

2:00 _____   _____

3:00 _____   _____

Recess/Lunch Duty Schedule: Below are the dates I have been assigned duty.

_____

Emergency Procedures

First Aid Kit: _____

Fire: _____

Natural disaster: _____

Class meeting place is: _____

If you have any questions, call Room _____ to talk with _____(buddy teacher).

Additional Activity Ideas:

1. _____   2. _____

3. _____   4. _____

5. _____

STUDENT RECORD SHEET

Name: _____

Age: _____

My birthday: _____

My teacher's name is _____.

Today's date is _____.

attach student
photo here

My favorite color is _____.

My favorite book is _____.

My favorite number is _____.

My favorite movie is _____.

My favorite song is _____.

My favorite ice cream flavor is _____.

My favorite sport is _____.

My hobbies are _____

_____

_____

I am good at _____

_____

_____

_____

I need to work on _____

_____

Student Award

Student

You did it! You met your goal of

You accomplished it by

Congratulations on your achievement!

Teacher

Date

94
reproducible